PAMELA J. THOMAS

Women Don't Retire

How to Pursue Your Passion and Leave Your Legacy

First published by Fiber of Life LLC 2025

Copyright © 2025 by Pamela J. Thomas

All rights reserved. No part of this publication may be reproduced, stored or transmitted in any form or by any means, electronic, mechanical, photocopying, recording, scanning, or otherwise without written permission from the publisher. It is illegal to copy this book, post it to a website, or distribute it by any other means without permission.

Pamela J. Thomas asserts the moral right to be identified as the author of this work.

Pamela J. Thomas has no responsibility for the persistence or accuracy of URLs for external or third-party Internet Websites referred to in this publication and does not guarantee that any content on such Websites is, or will remain, accurate or appropriate.

Designations used by companies to distinguish their products are often claimed as trademarks. All brand names and product names used in this book and on its cover are trade names, service marks, trademarks and registered trademarks of their respective owners. The publishers and the book are not associated with any product or vendor mentioned in this book. None of the companies referenced within the book have endorsed the book.

First edition

This book was professionally typeset on Reedsy.
Find out more at reedsy.com

Contents

Foreword   v
Preface   vii
Acknowledgments   ix
Introduction   1

I   Embracing Transition

1   Letter to My Sister   5
2   Letting Go of the Old Identity   7
3   Reclaiming Your Time & Energy   15
4   Navigating Uncertainty with Confidence   27
5   Spotlight: Faith in Transition   39

II   Designing Your Next Chapter

6   Letter to My Sister   47
7   Defining What Fulfillment Means to You   49
8   Spotlight: What I Wish I Knew   58
9   Exploring New Avenues for Impact   62
10   Financial Freedom: Beyond Mindset   75
11   Letter to My Sister   82

III   Building Community & Legacy

12   Sisterhood & Support: The Power of Connection   87
13   Letter to My Sister   96

14	Leaving a Legacy Beyond Work	98
15	Letter to My Sister	107
16	Embracing Joy, Play & Restorative Living	109
17	Spotlight: A Restorative Ritual for Wholeness	124
IV	Your Journey, Your Rules	
18	Letter to My Sister	131
19	Conclusion	133
	A Circle of Voices	139
	An Invitation	143
	About the Author	145
	Also by Pamela J. Thomas	150

Foreword

When I began my professional journey, there were no roadmaps for women like me—Black women determined to lead, build, and leave a lasting mark. We created our own paths, often through resistance and in rooms where we were the first, the only, and sometimes the last to be invited.

And when our titles changed—or disappeared altogether—no one handed us a guide for what comes next.

That's why this book, *Women Don't Retire*, is such a powerful and necessary offering. It speaks directly to a truth that I know deeply: for women of color, "retirement" isn't a stopping point. It's a threshold. It's a reimagining. It's a soulful return to the parts of ourselves we had to put on hold while we were busy breaking ceilings.

I believe that when one retires, it's important to retire to something. Otherwise, you start the next day with nothing to look forward to. The "something" you retire to can be something entirely new or something long left unfinished, so long as it gives purpose and meaning.

This book doesn't offer formulas—it offers *freedom*. It invites us to explore joy, rest, and alignment, not as a reward at the end of our service, but as the next chapter of our becoming. It doesn't tell us what to do—it asks who we're ready to be.

Pamela J. Thomas writes with the kind of wisdom that can only come from someone who has led with excellence and transitioned with grace. She brings a deep understanding of what it means to be a woman of color navigating the weight of leadership—and the beauty of what lies beyond it. Her words are gentle, strong, and timely. They remind us that we don't have to disappear when we step back—we get to *expand*.

This book is not just for those nearing retirement. It's for any woman standing at the edge of change. It's for the ones who are tired, the ones who are wondering what's next, and the ones who are quietly longing for more.

I am proud to add my voice to this work and to witness the continued legacy of women who choose to walk forward, soul first, truth intact, and legacy in motion.

This is not the end of your story. It is the beginning of something sacred.

Welcome to your next chapter.

— *Lillian Lincoln Lambert*
    Entrepreneur, Trailblazer, and Author of *The Road to Someplace Better*

Preface

This book began as a quiet nudge in my spirit—a gentle, persistent voice that said: *We need to talk about this.*

Not just about retirement. But about what comes *after* the role, the title, the long career. About what it means to be a woman of color who has given her all, made her mark, and now finds herself at a threshold no one prepared her for.

We are the first generation of women to arrive here in such numbers, with resources, with options, and with stories that stretch far beyond traditional narratives of "retirement." But so many of us arrive tired. Grieving. Uncertain. Or quietly wondering, *Who am I now that I'm not leading that team, solving those problems, showing up every day for everyone else?*

There's no blueprint for this part of the journey. At least, not one that honors our complexity. Our culture often focuses on achievement and hustle, legacy and leadership, but rarely on *letting go, resting, trusting, and transforming.* We don't talk enough about joy. Or about grief. Or about purpose beyond productivity.

This book is my offering to you—a companion for the sacred space you're stepping into. It's a guide, yes. But it's also a mirror. A conversation. A circle. A permission slip. It's a reminder that this season is not an end, but a *becoming.* That your wisdom, your creativity, your story, and your spirit are still unfolding in powerful, beautiful ways.

Women Don't Retire is not just a title. It's a truth we live. We evolve. We shift.

We reimagine. We keep showing up—sometimes softer, sometimes slower, but always deeper.

Whether you're standing at the edge of transition, in the thick of uncertainty, or already beginning to design your next chapter, I invite you to walk with me. To listen to your soul. To rest. To reflect. To dream again.

You are not done.

You are becoming more fully who you were always meant to be.

Welcome.

Acknowledgments

This book was born in the quiet spaces between endings and beginnings, between exhaustion and hope. And like all things meaningful in my life, it was not created alone.

To the women in my circle, thank you. You are my mirrors, my anchors, my laughter, my light. You have held space for me to become, again and again, and I carry your wisdom with me in every word on these pages.

To my family, your love has always made room for my dreaming. Thank you for believing in me when the way forward wasn't clear and for reminding me that purpose is not a destination, but a way of being.

To the women of color navigating transition with courage and curiosity—this book is for you. You are the reason I put pen to page. You are the reason I keep showing up. Your stories, your questions, your brilliance, and your softness inspired every chapter. Thank you for trusting me to name the things that often go unnamed.

To my mentors, teachers, and the ancestral voices who whispered guidance from beyond the veil—thank you. I feel your presence with me still.

To everyone who made space for this work to emerge—for the readers who showed up early, the editors who held the vision with care, and the communities who reminded me why this story matters—thank you for your partnership, your insight, and your sacred witnessing.

And finally, to Spirit—thank you for the still, small voice that never let me go. For the clarity that came when I made space. For the reminder that this work is not just mine, but part of something greater.

May this offering serve as a light, a mirror, and a gentle invitation home.

With gratitude beyond words,

Pam

Introduction

You stand at the peak of your career, having poured your heart and soul into building a path that reflects your dedication and resilience. After decades of hard work, you've hit those significant milestones that matter to you. You cherish the work you do and are deeply invested in the success of your organization and community.

Yet, as you look ahead, you may find yourself approaching or even crossing into a new phase—the post-career chapter of your life. This transition can feel daunting, leaving you with a sense of unease about stepping away from the corporate world that has defined so much of your identity.

While it's essential to have a solid financial plan as you navigate this phase, the more pressing question looms larger: "What will I do with my life now?"

Instead of letting uncertainty immobilize you, consider embracing this moment as a chance to redefine your future. Retirement is not an end; it's an opportunity to pursue your passions, clarify your purpose, and leave a lasting legacy in your community and beyond!

There's no need to postpone your dreams simply because you're unsure of how to transition smoothly. If you've been pondering what comes next and feeling anxious about the future, this book is crafted just for you.

This guide is for those who seek meaningful and impactful retirement planning, specifically tailored for women of color who have navigated unique challenges and triumphs throughout their careers.

Many assume they're ready for retirement simply because they've saved, but often, they find that they've only prepared financially. Others might face an unexpected early retirement, realizing they have no plan at all. Are you ready to stop ruminating and start taking actionable steps to design your ideal retirement life?

Yes, you need a solid succession plan for your work. Still, it's equally vital to cultivate a retirement strategy that ensures not just financial security, but also personal fulfillment and joy.

While the idea of planning may not initially excite you, it can be a profoundly creative process. The more we succeed in our careers, the more our lives can become one-dimensional. Retirement planning offers a chance to rediscover those aspects of ourselves that may have been overshadowed by work obligations.

You'll never regret investing time in planning for your retirement. The clarity and peace of mind that come from having a plan are truly invaluable.

Remember, a plan isn't the final answer; it's merely a starting point. Think of it as a framework that will guide you through the challenges and changes you'll encounter as you transition into a vibrant new way of life. Your legacy awaits—let's embark on this journey together!

I

Embracing Transition

Transition isn't an end—it's a sacred return to yourself. This season invites you to slow down, release old roles, and rediscover who you're becoming. It's not about having all the answers, but making space to listen deeply. Here, we honor the pause, embrace the unknown, and step into a new chapter with grace, clarity, and courage.

1

Letter to My Sister

To the Sister Standing at the Edge

"You may not know what's next, and that's okay. Standing at the edge means you're still brave enough to change. You are not lost—you are listening."

Dear Sister,

You may not know what's next, and that's okay.

Standing at the edge of change can feel like standing on sacred ground. It's where fear and hope sit side by side, where grief mingles with possibility. Where the old version of you begins to loosen her grip, and the new one hasn't quite arrived.

I want you to know: you are not lost—you are listening.

This moment, right here, is holy. It is not weakness that brought you to this edge—it is wisdom. The wisdom to pause. The courage to stop running long enough to ask, *What do I want now? Who am I without the title, the role, the expectations?*

It's okay if the answers aren't clear yet. Clarity rarely arrives all at once. Often, it comes in whispers—found in quiet mornings, unexpected tears, a flash of joy that reminds you you're still alive and becoming.

Let go of the need to know everything. You're not behind. You're not broken. You're simply in transition, and that is both brave and beautiful.

This is not the end of your story. It's the beginning of a new chapter—one that you get to write on your terms.

So take a deep breath. Stand tall. Trust yourself. And when you're ready, take that next small step forward.

With love and deep belief in your becoming,

Your Sister in Transition

2

Letting Go of the Old Identity

"It can be painful to let go of the things we believe define us. But releasing them makes space for our inner wisdom to emerge and transform our lives."

The Emotional Challenges of Leaving Leadership

Almost 25 years ago, I made a decision that changed the course of my life—I walked away from my corporate career. At the time, I was one of the few Black women in executive leadership. On paper, I had it all: the business trips, the corner office, access to influential people, and a well-connected network. But deep down, I knew something was missing.

You see, I've always had a unique way of looking at the world. I move to my own rhythm, and that has always been my strength. It helped me navigate corporate spaces where I often found myself as the only woman of color in the room. But no matter how much success I achieved, I couldn't shake the feeling that I was playing a role rather than living my truth. I wasn't able to fully express my cultural identity in that environment, and that, more than anything, left me feeling disconnected.

It wasn't just about me, either. I kept asking myself, 'What am I really contributing to my community?' How am I making a difference for people who look like me? No matter how many promotions I earned, that question continued to nag at me. Eventually, I realized that I needed to step out of that world and find work that aligned with my values and allowed me to have a real impact.

Walking away wasn't easy. It was terrifying. Corporate life, despite its limitations, offers structure, a steady income, and a built-in support system. When I left, all of that disappeared overnight. I went from having a team around me, all working toward common goals, to sitting alone with nothing but my thoughts and a big question mark about what came next. I had fought hard to get to where I was, and suddenly, I had to start over. As much as I wanted independence, I quickly learned that freedom comes with its own price, especially for women like me, who are used to navigating complex systems to have a seat at the table.

The Reckoning

There's a moment in every woman's journey when the mask begins to slip. When the title, the accolades, the busy calendar, and the identity we've worn so well start to feel... heavy. Ill-fitting. Even unfamiliar.

For women of color who have spent decades in leadership, this unraveling can feel disorienting. After all, we've often had to be twice as good, twice as prepared, and twice as composed. We earned our place at the table through grit and grace. But what happens when we're ready to leave the table? Or to build a new one?

We're mourning the loss of a role that defined us, not because we were small, but because we were so good at being who the world needed us to be. Leadership shaped how we navigated the world, how others responded to us, and even how we perceived ourselves.

Many of us have spent decades shaping ourselves to fit systems that weren't designed with our full humanity in mind. The pressure to be competent, composed, and unquestionable isn't just internal—it's systemic. Elizabeth Leiba names this tension plainly in her book, *I Came to Slay: The Black Girl's Guide to Conquering Every Battle*:

> *In **I'm Not Yelling**, I redefine impostor syndrome as "impostor treatment" because the feelings of self-doubt many of us experience aren't about who we are—they're about how we've been treated in spaces that weren't designed for us. These doubts are reactions to systemic bias and exclusion, not personal flaws."*

These words echo the quiet fatigue so many of us feel—and rarely say aloud. When we talk about letting go of identity, we're not just talking about stepping away from a job. We're talking about releasing the performance of safety, the code-switching, the constant need to anticipate how we're being perceived. Letting go is not failure—it's freedom.

Letting go of an identity shaped in these environments isn't easy. But it's also what frees us to trust ourselves again. To build a new identity from within, rather than from performance.

Letting go is rarely just logistical—it's emotional. It stirs grief, confusion, and unexpected pain. And yet, within that pain is the invitation to heal.

> *"We must have the courage to share our pain in order to free ourselves."*
> —Nemonte Nenquimo, Waorani Indigenous leader and activist

What we name, we can release. What we feel, we can move through. You don't have to carry it alone, but you do have to acknowledge it.

Letting go doesn't mean forgetting or erasing all that we've accomplished. It means loosening our grip on the identity we constructed to survive—and beginning to uncover the one that was always waiting to thrive.

This season calls us inward. It calls us to listen not to what's expected of us, but to what's *emerging* from us. What does your soul want now? What brings you peace? What feels aligned, even if it makes no sense to the outside world?

Letting go can feel like loss, but it's also the beginning of liberation. When we no longer have to perform, we begin to feel. When we stop chasing approval, we begin to hear our intuition again.

You don't need to rush into what's next. You only need to be honest about what is now. This is your sacred threshold. This is where the next version of you begins.

Let go. You're not falling. You're finally landing in yourself.

Honoring Your Career While Moving Forward

Letting go of a role that has defined you is more than just an external shift—it's an internal reckoning. It's about acknowledging all that you've given and sacrificed, and all the ways your career molded your sense of self. There is grief in that process, even when the decision to walk away is yours.

But here's what I learned: it's possible to honor that chapter of your life without being bound to it. The strength, resilience, and brilliance that brought you to leadership don't go away when you leave the title behind. Those qualities are still yours to carry forward.

I began to understand that the essence of leadership—the drive to serve, influence, and create change—could manifest in various forms. Leadership didn't have to be tied to a job description. It could be community-based, rooted in mentoring, or expressed through writing, healing, or teaching.

Redefining Who You Are

At the heart of letting go is a question we often avoid: *Who am I without the role?* For women of color who've had to work twice as hard to prove their value, this question can feel particularly destabilizing. Our professional achievements have often been our armor, our validation, our proof that we belong.

This process takes time. It's not linear. Some days, you'll feel empowered by the possibilities ahead. Other days, you may mourn the routine, recognition, or influence you once had. And that's okay.

For me, it helped to see this transition not as a fall, but as a turning point. It was an invitation to rediscover the parts of me that had been muted for too long. It was a chance to ask: *What do I want now? What brings me joy, peace, and fulfillment, outside of career accomplishments?*

Case Study: Lisa's Journey from CEO to Community Mentor

Lisa spent over 30 years climbing the corporate ladder. She was the go-to person for high-stakes decisions, the mentor for younger executives, and the face of her company's success. When she stepped away, she felt invisible.

"I no longer had a calendar full of meetings or an inbox full of urgent emails," she said. "At first, it felt like freedom. Then, it felt like I was drifting."

Lisa eventually found a new purpose in mentoring other women transitioning out of leadership. She started a small coaching group, sharing her experiences and helping others navigate their own journeys. Over time, she realized that her identity wasn't tied to her position—it was tied to her ability to uplift and guide others, just in a new way.

Her story is a powerful reminder: your purpose doesn't disappear when you leave your job. It evolves.

The Emotional Landscape of Transition

What no one tells you is that stepping away from your career can feel like stepping into an emotional minefield. There's grief, doubt, guilt, and sometimes even shame—especially if people around you don't understand why you left or think you should still be "doing more."

And yet, there's also relief. There's space. There's silence that allows you to hear yourself again.

In this silence, you might rediscover passions you shelved years ago. You might find that what truly lights you up has nothing to do with boardrooms or performance reviews.

Maybe it's storytelling. Maybe it's gardening. Maybe it's advocacy, or painting, or rest.

The emotional work of letting go is sacred. It's what allows us to release the internalized belief that our worth is tied to productivity.

As you begin to release roles, expectations, and identities, remember:

> "Breathe. Let go. And remind yourself that this very moment is the only one you know you have for sure."
> —Oprah Winfrey

Journaling Prompt: What Are You Ready to Release?

Take a moment to reflect on the aspects of your leadership identity that still serve you and the ones that no longer fit. Write about:

- What aspects of my career brought me the most fulfillment?
- What parts of my identity feel difficult to let go of, and why?
- How can I honor my past while making space for my future?
- Who am I becoming now?

Letting go is not about erasing the past; it's about making room for something new. This chapter is just the beginning of redefining who you are beyond the title, beyond the job description, beyond what you thought retirement was supposed to be.

And trust me, there is power in this pause. There is strength in asking, *Who am I now?* And there is so much possibility waiting on the other side of that question.

3

Reclaiming Your Time & Energy

"Balance is not perfection—it's presence. It's found in the spaces between expansion and contraction, effort and stillness, like the wings of a bird in flight."

Redefining Time on Your Terms

In our careers, our calendars often ruled our lives. Meetings, deadlines, travel—it all gave structure to our days. For many women of color, the corporate world demanded not just our time, but our constant vigilance. Time wasn't our own; it was a resource we gave away in service of goals that didn't always nourish us.

Now that you're stepping into a new season, you have the radical opportunity to reclaim your time. And let me tell you—it's a beautiful, sometimes bewildering, process.

We're so conditioned to be productive that rest can feel like a guilty indulgence.

Leisure can feel like laziness. And open time? That can feel like a void. But here's the truth: how we use our time reflects what we truly value. This new chapter presents an opportunity to be intentional about what matters most.

Structure Without Rigidity

Some people thrive with a rigid routine. Others need freedom and spontaneity. Most of us need something in between. One of the best gifts you can give yourself is a rhythm that flows with your life, not against it.

Instead of replicating the high-intensity pace of your career, ask yourself: What does a nourishing day look like? What practices help me feel grounded? Where can I make space for joy, connection, and rest?

Structure doesn't have to mean tight schedules. It can mean setting boundaries around your mornings, dedicating afternoons to your creative projects, or reserving evenings for family time. It's about being deliberate, not dogmatic.

And don't be surprised if, at first, your sense of time feels unmoored. That's common in the early days of transition. Your body and mind are still operating on a corporate clock. Give yourself grace as you adjust. Think of it as jet lag from a long-haul flight—except this time, you're arriving in a destination you've chosen.

The Value of Leisure

In retirement, leisure isn't just a luxury—it's a tool for renewal. But we have to redefine what leisure means.

It's not just about Netflix binges or idle time. It's about creating spaciousness in your life. Time to reflect. Time to be present. Time to explore passions you shelved for years.

When you give yourself permission to enjoy your time, you begin to shift your relationship with it. You stop seeing rest as wasted potential and start seeing it as essential to your well-being.

This might mean taking long walks with no destination. Sitting with a book you've wanted to read for years. Learning to paint, or cook, or dance. Leisure is not the opposite of value—it is where we often reconnect with our most authentic selves.

Rebalancing Your Energy

Energy is as valuable as time, and often, we don't notice where ours is going until we feel drained. In this next chapter, think of yourself as the steward of your energy.

Ask:

- What activities energize me?
- What drains me?
- Who are the people who uplift me?
- What commitments no longer align with my values?

Your "no" is sacred. Your "yes" should be aligned with joy, not obligation. We are not meant to be endlessly available, especially not during a life stage that is intended for healing and purpose.

And don't forget to honor your physical energy, too. Your body is wiser than you think. It may need more sleep, more movement, more stillness. Listen to it. Trust it. Care for it like the vessel of your legacy.

* * *

<u>Reclaiming Rhythm After Burnout</u>

Burnout has a way of leaving echoes in the body long after the crisis has passed.

It's not just about being tired. It's about being disconnected from yourself, from joy, from the quiet pulse of your own inner rhythm. After years of pushing, proving, overextending, and showing up for everyone else, you may find yourself in a strange silence when the urgency finally stops.

Many women don't realize how deeply burnout alters their sense of time, energy, and identity. We get used to running on adrenaline. We stop listening to what we need because we've been conditioned to ignore it.

Our calendars ruled our lives. Our obligations masked our exhaustion. Even our moments of rest were often filled with guilt.

And now, here you are. No longer on that hamster wheel. But also not quite sure what it means to slow down.

Not sure what it means to truly rest.

This is where rhythm comes in.

Why Rhythm Matters

Rhythm is not routine. It's not a strict schedule. It's the natural flow of your life—the rise and fall of your energy, your moods, your needs. It's the wisdom of the body that says, I need movement today, or I need stillness, or I need joy. Rhythm honors that wisdom.

When you reclaim your rhythm, you begin to listen again. You start to create a life that supports you, rather than forcing yourself to support a life that no longer fits.

This is healing work. And it's slow work. But it is sacred.

Our energy expands and contracts like breath. Balance isn't fixed—it's dynamic.

"Your hand opens and closes, opens and closes. If it were always a fist or always stretched open, you would be paralysed... the two as beautifully balanced and coordinated as birds' wings."
— Rumi

Listening to the Body's Clock

One of the first steps to finding your rhythm again is listening to your body. Our bodies hold incredible wisdom, but burnout teaches us to ignore it. Now is the time to reintroduce yourself to your signals.

Ask yourself:

- *When does my energy naturally rise and fall during the day?*
- *How does my body feel after I spend time with certain people or do certain tasks?*
- *What sensations tell me I need to rest? To eat? To move? To create?*
- *Keeping a daily log—even for just one week—can offer powerful insight into your natural rhythm. You'll begin to notice patterns. Honor those. Adjust your days gradually to align with your truth.*

You are not a machine. You are cyclical, seasonal, sacred...

Creating Anchors, Not Schedules

Instead of rigid routines, consider creating anchors for your day, touchpoints that help ground and restore you. These might include:

- A morning walk before checking your phone
- A quiet moment with tea and a blessing at midday
- A sunset gratitude practice
- An early bedtime with a calming ritual
- Turning off screens at a particular hour each night

Rest As Rhythm, Not Rescue

In a life of burnout, rest was always delayed. It came only after collapse. It was reactive, not rhythmic.

But what if rest became a part of your rhythm? What if it wasn't something you earned, but something you built your life around?

You don't have to wait until you're drained to restore yourself. Rest can be infused into every part of the day:

- Pausing between tasks
- Eating slowly and with presence
- Lying down in the middle of the day without guilt
- Saying "no" when your body says "enough"
- This is the revolutionary act: choosing rest as a way of being.

Spiritual Rhythm

Reclaiming rhythm isn't just physical—it's spiritual. Many of us have lost our connection to ritual, sacred pause, and soulful stillness.

You might begin to explore:

- *Moon phases and how they influence your emotions and energy*
- *Sabbath days or hours each week, where no productivity is required*
- *Sacred journaling, where you ask Spirit, What do I need today?*
- *Monthly "reset" days, to align with your values and vision*

Rhythm connects you to yourself— but also to something greater. It reminds you that you are not meant to give constantly. You are meant to receive.

Reflection: What Rhythm Feels Like

As you begin to rebuild your rhythm, come back to how you want to feel. Ask yourself:

1. *What does "ease" feel like in my body?*
2. *What practices help me return to that feeling?*
3. *What makes me feel heavy? What lifts me?*
4. *What kind of pace honors who I am now?*

Your rhythm may not make sense to anyone else. And that's okay. You are not building a schedule — you are building a sanctuary.

Let each day become a prayer.

Let your rhythm be your recovery.

* * *

Rebuilding from Within

When I left corporate life, I was eager for freedom, but I didn't anticipate the emotional toll of unstructured time. Without meetings, deadlines, or a packed calendar, I had to relearn how to navigate my day. I had to rebuild how I used my time from the ground up.

It started with small rituals: morning walks, midday journaling, weekly check-ins with myself. These became the anchors that allowed me to shape a life with meaning. Not one dictated by others, but one rooted in how I wanted to feel each day.

Eventually, I realized that my days didn't need to be packed to be meaningful. What mattered was that they were mine. That they reflected my values and supported my wholeness.

That's the essence of this chapter: to make space for yourself not just in your schedule, but in your spirit. To allow yourself the time to become, to grieve, to celebrate, and to reimagine.

The Rhythm of Renewal

The more profound truth about reclaiming time and energy is that it's really about creating rhythm—your rhythm. In our careers, our pace was often set by others. The calendar was full of "shoulds." This new season invites you to tune in to your natural rhythms. What time of day are you most creative? When do you feel most peaceful?

Some women in retirement begin to live by the moon, syncing their intentions with new and full moons as a way to connect to divine timing. Others adopt seasonal rhythms, embracing winter as a time of rest and introspection.

These gentle cycles remind us: life isn't a race. It's a rhythm. And you get to dance in your tempo now.

The Cultural Work of Slowing Down

For many women of color, slowing down is not just a personal decision—it's a cultural reclamation. We have inherited generations of overwork, sacrifice, and survival. Rest and spaciousness often feel unfamiliar, even dangerous.

We are not always granted the luxury of resting without scrutiny. For women of color—especially those of us who have held it all together in boardrooms, in church pews, and around kitchen tables—choosing rest can feel like a radical act. Not because we don't need it, but because the world often demands that we keep going no matter what. The minute we choose ourselves, step back, say no, or simply stop moving, the questions start. The assumptions roll in. The attacks, even subtle ones, come cloaked in concern or curiosity. Michelle Obama recently spoke to this very tension in a conversation with Sophia Bush:

> "That's the thing that we as women struggle with: disappointing people. I mean, so much so that this year, people couldn't even fathom that I was making a choice for myself. That they had to assume that my husband and I are divorcing."
> — Michelle Obama, Work in Progress podcast

Her words struck a chord. They reminded me that, despite all her accomplishments, influence, and visibility, she is not exempt from the same narratives that haunt so many of us: that choosing yourself means abandoning others, that setting boundaries is selfish, or that rest must come at a cost. But we know better. Choosing rest is not the end of our story—it is the beginning of our return to ourselves.

Your rest is an act of healing. Your joy is a resistance song. When you refuse to grind yourself into the ground, you interrupt a cycle. You create a new possibility for the generations that follow.

This is not just about *your* time. It's about reimagining time for everyone. You are modeling a new way to live. One rooted in enoughness. In grace. In liberation.

Planning Your Time with Intention

If you want your time to reflect what matters, it helps to plan—not with rigidity, but with care and consideration. Create space each week to set intentions. Ask:

- What's one thing I want to prioritize for my well-being?
- What's one connection I want to nurture?
- What creative or purposeful activity will I explore?

You don't need to fill every hour. But choosing how to engage with your time gives you agency. It makes life feel spacious, not scattered.

You might even consider creating themed days. One day a week could be your "creative" day, another your "community" day. The goal isn't to control your life—it's to honor it.

Wisdom from the Journey

Let this next chapter be one where you take up space—not just physically, but energetically and spiritually. You don't need to shrink to accommodate others. Your presence is not too much.

> *"Don't take a backward step. Don't shy away from taking up space in the world."*
> —Dr. Ngozi Okonjo-Iweala, Nigerian economist and WTO Director-General

Spaciousness is not selfish. It is the condition in which your soul gets to breathe and expand.

The Delany Sisters (Sadie and Bessie, the centenarians) put it even more plainly: *"Keep your own calendar. The most important thing in your life is your time."*

We've worked too hard, for too long, to hand our time over to other people's agendas. This is your moment to reclaim it.

And this doesn't mean you won't be busy—it means you get to choose the busy that aligns with your soul.

Journaling Prompt: Designing Your Ideal Day

Sketch out your ideal day. Not a fantasy—but a grounded, nourishing, joyful day in this season of life. Include:

- Morning rituals
- Movement and rest
- Connection with others
- Time for creativity, exploration, or purpose

Then take one small step toward making that day your reality.

Final Thought

Time is not just a resource—it's your life. How you spend it shapes who you become.

And in this chapter, you get to decide what that looks like. Give yourself permission to slow down. To savor. To say no. To say yes to the things that feed your soul.

This is your time. You've earned it. Now let it be yours in every sense of the word.

4

Navigating Uncertainty with Confidence

"Crossing thresholds is rarely linear. It's more like a dance—two steps forward, one step back, a twirl of confusion, a leap of faith."

Embracing the Threshold

Retirement isn't just a destination—it's a threshold. And thresholds can be intimidating places. You're no longer where you were, but not quite where you're going. For many women of color, this space feels both unfamiliar and vulnerable. We've spent so long building careers, managing expectations, and carrying the weight of representation that stepping away from that identity can feel like losing our ground.

But here's the beauty of thresholds: they are spaces of potential—the place where old definitions fall away and new possibilities emerge.

This period of your life may feel uncertain, and that's okay. Uncertainty doesn't mean you're lost. It means you're in the midst of transformation.

The Emotional Landscape of Transition

We particularly want to avoid the emotional aspects of crossing the threshold. There is a grieving process that we must navigate. We are mourning the end of an essential part of our lives. As women of color, we often carry the weight of expectations from our families, our communities, and ourselves.

When facing transitions, especially retirement, it's crucial to acknowledge the emotional terrain:

- Grief for the roles and identities we're leaving behind
- Anxiety about the unknown future
- Excitement for new possibilities
- Pressure to succeed or "represent" our communities
- Relief from stepping away from systemic challenges we've faced

Allowing ourselves to experience these emotions fully is part of the journey. It's okay to mourn the end of one chapter even as we look forward to the next.

The Liminal Space: Where Growth Begins

In anthropological terms, this in-between phase is referred to as *liminality*. It's the disorienting, often uncomfortable, place between what was and what will be. We've experienced it before—graduating from school, changing careers, becoming mothers, ending relationships.

Now, you're in a liminal space again.

It's tempting to rush through it, to grasp for clarity. But the in-between is where creativity lives. It's where you begin to ask, *What do I want now? Who am I becoming?*

When we resist the urge to find quick answers and allow the unknown to shape us, something powerful happens: we begin to redefine ourselves from the inside out.

> "The only thing constant in the world is change, that's why today I take life as it comes."
> —India Arie

Avoiding Quick Fixes

In moments of uncertainty, it's tempting to grasp for quick solutions. We might:

- Throw ourselves into new projects without reflection
- Cling to outdated identities or roles
- Seek comfort in unhealthy habits or relationships

When we reach for something from a place of fear, we often become attached to what no longer serves us. Instead, we can choose to sit with the discomfort, knowing that it's a sign of growth and transformation. We don't have to figure it all out at once. We just have to stay present.

Letting Your Inner Wisdom Lead

In times of uncertainty, the temptation is to look outward for answers—advice from friends, reassurance from others, and validation from external success. But this chapter calls you inward.

Your inner wisdom has been with you all along. The part of you that has made tough decisions, trusted your gut, weathered storms, and helped others find their way. She is still there. Still wise. Still available to guide you.

Transitions are never linear. But even in the dark, we are guided.

> "Light always returns. Even in the darkest hour, light finds a way."
> —Iyanla Vanzant

Build a practice of listening:

- Spend five minutes each morning asking, *What do I need today?*
- End the week with a reflection: *Where did I feel aligned? Where did I feel off-track?*
- Ask yourself: *What would I do if I trusted myself completely?*

These small acts of self-dialogue strengthen your confidence and return you to your center.

Building Confidence Through Reflection

Confidence in this new phase doesn't come from external achievements—it comes from deep listening and radical trust.

Here are some questions to help build that foundation:

- What do I truly desire in this next chapter?
- What have I learned about myself through past transitions?
- What qualities do I carry that will support me now?
- Where have I been resilient, and what have I learned from that experience?

Confidence grows when we recognize our resourcefulness. You've navigated complex environments. You've adapted. You've succeeded. Now, you have everything you need to do it again—on your own terms.

When We Change at Different Speeds – Navigating Transition in Relationships

One of the quieter complexities of transition is this: we don't all go through it the same way, at the same time, or with the same emotional language. And when we love people—partners, friends, siblings—who are also in transition or not yet in transition, the gap between us can feel wide.

Many women experience retirement or career shifts as an emotional and spiritual reckoning. It's not just about not working anymore—it's about letting go of roles that once defined us, rediscovering who we are without the title, and wondering what purpose feels like now. It's tender, sometimes lonely, and often confusing.

For men, retirement may be more task-oriented. They may look forward to rest, hobbies, or a break from professional pressure. However, they may also struggle with the loss of control, structure, or identity, without having the tools or language to cope with it. Their approach might seem more practical and less emotional. Sometimes more solitary. Or even avoidant.

These differences are not about right or wrong. They're about rhythm and roles. But when we're not mindful of them, they can create misunderstanding, resentment, or emotional distance.

Common Differences in Navigating Transition

Transition does not speak in one language. It whispers through emotion, identity, purpose, and pace, and how we interpret it is often shaped by gendered expectations.

Many women, especially those raised to nurture and connect, tend to process transitions in relationships. They reach out, seek emotional language, and lean into community for support. For them, change may awaken a deeper grieving process—one that mourns the loss of purpose or identity, especially if their roles have been tied to caregiving or leadership.

In contrast, many men, socialized to be independent and in control, may approach transition in solitude. They often feel pressure to "figure it out" on their own, and may struggle to name or openly explore their emotions. Instead of grieving the loss of identity, they may zero in on the loss of productivity, structure, or control. Where women might seek spiritual or soul-aligned guidance, men may default to distraction, staying busy, or anchoring themselves in routine as a means of coping.

This isn't about binaries or placing one approach above another. Instead, it's about recognizing the cultural scripts many of us inherit—and how those scripts either support or complicate the process of personal growth and evolution. Women may be more ready to recreate themselves and reimagine a new chapter. Men, meanwhile, may feel hesitant or uncertain, not because they lack vision, but because they've rarely been invited to imagine beyond their roles.

Understanding these differences helps us hold space for one another with greater compassion and understanding. It reminds us that there is no one "right" way to navigate change—only the way that honors who we are truly becoming.

When One Partner Grows First

Sometimes, you begin to grow and shift before your partner does. You may want to explore your thoughts more deeply, dream differently, and reimagine your rhythm. You may crave joy, rest, or creativity, but you're still anchored to routine or unsure how to connect.

This can be hard.

It can feel like you're speaking different emotional languages. Or worse, like one of you is ready to evolve and the other is standing still. But change doesn't always happen in tandem. Your growth can still be an invitation, not a threat.

And often, women carry the invisible burden of trying to make the transition easier for everyone. We worry about how our growth will affect the people we love. We delay our rest or mute our dreams so we don't disrupt the household or unsettle the relationship. As Jerome Myers, author of Exit to Excellence, wisely observed:

> *"The intention for women is to get everybody through to the other side without anybody being harmed, and they're willing to compromise and sacrifice in a lot of ways to keep the peace and make everybody happy."*

This tendency to protect others at our own expense is deeply rooted. But this season asks something different. It invites us to honor our own becoming without abandoning connection. To trust that honesty, not harmony at all costs, is what allows real intimacy to grow.

I've witnessed countless moments like the one below—two people, facing similar uncertainty, but responding in very different ways. This conversation reflects some of the common ways men and women tend to process change, shaped not only by personality but also by deeper cultural conditioning.

"I just need a plan," he said, rubbing his hands together like he was revving an engine. "If I can map out the next steps, I'll be fine. Sitting in this space, it's just not productive."

She nodded, but her eyes were soft with something else entirely. "I need to talk it through," she said quietly. "Not just the logistics—the feelings. I don't even know who I am anymore. I've poured so much of myself into that role."

He looked away for a moment. "I get that. I just... I wouldn't even know how to start with all that. Talking about it makes it real, you know?"

"Exactly," she replied. "That's the point. I need it to be real so I can move through it. Otherwise, I'll just stay stuck."

He offered a half-smile. "For me, it's easier to stay busy. Go to the gym, check off a list, do something—anything. That's how I know I'm still okay."

"And I light candles," she said, laughing gently. "I sit with my journal, or call a friend who knows how to hold space. That's how I find what's next—by listening inward first."

These are not opposites. They're reflections of how we've been taught to cope—how our stories have been shaped by gender, culture, and expectation. One reaches for structure. The other reaches for soul. Both are seeking ground.

What matters is not whose way is better. What matters is permission—permission to grieve, to pause, to ask for help, to begin again. In our rhythm. In our voice.

How to Stay Connected Through the Shift

- **Name what's happening.** Let your loved one know that this season is shifting you, not in a way that pulls you away, but that calls you inward. Invite them into that awareness.
- **Don't demand sameness.** It's okay if your journeys look different. It's okay if they don't understand yet. Model what alignment looks like without insisting they match it.
- **Create rituals of connection.** These might be simple—walks, conversations, cooking together—but they ground the relationship in shared presence.
- **Invite, don't convince.** Share what you're learning or longing for, not as a correction, but as a window into your world.
- **Get support.** Couples therapy, spiritual direction, men's circles, or peer groups can help both people navigate the shift without carrying it alone.

Reflection Questions

- Where do I feel seen and supported in my close relationships at the moment?
- What emotional language do I need from my partner, and have I asked for it directly?
- What assumptions am I making about how they're experiencing this transition?
- Where am I growing, and how can I invite loved ones into that growth with grace?

This not only honors your personal journey—it gives you tools to protect, evolve, and enrich the relationships you value most.

Support Systems and the Power of Community

You don't have to navigate this threshold alone. You shouldn't. Community, sisterhood, mentorship—these aren't luxuries; they're essentials.

The journey is easier when we have partners and advisors to share our ups and downs. It's really about having the right people to help you see what you can't see, challenge assumptions, discover new truths, encourage, care, and assist in any way possible to help get you through your waiting.

Look for:

- Women who have redefined retirement on their own terms
- Inter-generational connections that offer diverse perspectives
- Spaces that celebrate and understand your cultural background
- Professional networks that can guide financial and career transitions

When you surround yourself with people who see your potential—especially when you can't see it yet—you begin to believe in new possibilities.

Creating Rituals for Transitions

Transitions are sacred. One way to bring depth and intention to your season of change is through ritual.

Try:

- A letting-go ceremony where you write and release the old titles, identities, or fears you are ready to release
- A grounding ritual each morning: light a candle, speak a blessing, affirm your worth
- A personal affirmation practice: "I am growing, even when I feel uncertain."

Rituals offer a sense of meaning and stability when life feels unsteady. They mark your transition not as a loss, but as an opening.

Redirecting Your Energy

Let's be clear: this isn't about stopping. It's about redirecting your energy and wisdom.

Retirement might mean:

- Starting a business that serves your community
- Mentoring the next generation of leaders

- Pursuing educational opportunities you didn't have earlier in life
- Engaging in activism and community service
- Exploring creative passions you've long deferred

Journaling Prompt: Confidence in the In-Between

Write about a time when you navigated uncertainty and came through stronger. Then reflect:

- What strengths did I lean on during that time?
- What did I learn about myself?
- How can I apply that wisdom now?

Let this be your reminder: the in-between is not a void. It's a space brimming with potential. It's a sacred place of becoming.

And you—you are more than equipped to walk through it with grace, strength, and confidence.

5

Spotlight: Faith in Transition

There are moments when plans fall apart, timelines shift, and everything looks different from what we expected. And if we're honest, transition can shake the very foundation upon which we've built our lives. It invites uncertainty, stirs old fears, and asks us to trust what we cannot yet see. This is where faith becomes more than belief—it becomes a way of being.

Faith doesn't always mean religion. It can be prayer, intuition, energy, or a connection to something greater. It's that inner knowing that whispers, *even now, I am held.* It's what keeps us moving when logic tells us to stop. It's what gives us peace when there's no map, no clarity, no control.

If you're in a season where your former identity is fading and the next one hasn't fully emerged, you're not alone. These "in-between" places, the wilderness of transition, are not punishments. They are sacred invitations to deepen your faith.

Letting Go of Control

Many of us have survived by staying in control, planning, preparing, and performing. We mapped out our careers, managed crises, and held our families down. But transition is not a space where control thrives. It's a space where *surrender* becomes the path.

Surrender doesn't mean giving up. It means loosening our grip so something greater can enter. It means trusting that what is leaving is making room for something more aligned with your purpose.

Letting go is a spiritual practice. You release the need to know everything. You release the urgency to fix. You stop forcing and start allowing.

It is in surrender that peace enters.

When the Old Answers Don't Work Anymore

One of the hardest parts of this season is realizing that what once sustained you might not serve you anymore. The affirmations, routines, and beliefs that got you through the early phases of life may feel too small now.

You may even find yourself questioning the spiritual truths you held onto tightly. That's not failure—it's evolution. Faith is not stagnant. It grows with us. Sometimes, it breaks open so something deeper can rise.

In these moments, don't rush to fill the silence. Sit with it. Ask your spirit what it needs at this moment. Listen for new language, new rhythms, new truths.

Your faith is still yours. It's just stretching to meet the size of your becoming.

Spiritual Practices for Grounding

When the ground beneath you feels shaky, grounding practices reconnect you to what's true. Here are a few that have supported women in transition:

- **Breath prayers** – Simple, sacred words you repeat with your inhale and exhale
- **Walking meditations** – Movement with presence, especially in nature
- **Gratitude lists** – A daily reminder of what's still holding you
- **Lighting a candle** – As a symbol of light, presence, or divine guidance
- **Scripture, poetry, or devotionals** – Texts that feed your spirit, no matter their source

These aren't about perfection. They're about presence. About saying, *I'm here. I'm listening. I trust what's unfolding, even if I don't understand it yet.*

Faith as Legacy

Many of us inherited our faith from mothers and grandmothers who prayed us through. Who laid hands on our heads. Who lit candles in silence. Whether they spoke it or not, their faith was a blueprint.

Now, you get to shape your own. You get to keep what's true, release what no longer fits, and pass on a version of faith rooted in wholeness, not fear.

Maybe that means sharing your spiritual journey with your children. Or creating rituals for your grandchildren. Or simply living in a way that reflects grace, trust, and reverence for life.

Your faith, lived authentically, becomes part of your legacy.

When Doubt Creeps In

Let's be real—faith isn't constant—doubt visits. We wonder if we missed the sign. If the silence means we're alone. If we've strayed too far from the path.

Let me assure you: doubt is part of the process. It doesn't cancel your faith—it expands it.

God can handle your questions. Spirit doesn't shrink away from your honesty. You are allowed to wrestle, to weep, to waver. What matters is that you don't stop seeking. That you continue to show up with a heart open to guidance.

Sometimes the most faithful act is simply staying open.

Words to Anchor You

Here are a few words you can return to when you need grounding:

- *Even in this, I am not alone.*
- *I trust the timing of my life.*
- *I release what no longer serves me.*
- *I am safe to rest. I am safe to grow.*
- *My path is unfolding with grace.*

Repeat them like mantras. Write them on mirrors. Whisper them in the morning. Let them become a soundtrack of your transformation.

Faith as Fuel for What's Next

Eventually, the fog begins to lift. The path becomes clearer. The next version of your purpose begins to rise. And it's your faith—the quiet trust you held onto in the dark—that fuels your movement forward.

Faith doesn't mean you never feel fear. It means you keep moving, even with trembling hands.

It's the bridge between who you've been and who you're becoming.

And Sister, who you're becoming is sacred.

II

Designing Your Next Chapter

This is your time to create a life that reflects your truth. Designing your next chapter means leading with joy, clarity, and purpose—not obligation. It's about dreaming freely, choosing boldly, and shaping each day around what matters most to you now.

6

Letter to My Sister

To the Sister Who's Letting Go

"You've held so much for so long. It's okay to set it down. You do not lose yourself by letting go. You meet yourself there."

Dear Sister,

I see you in the tender moment of release.

You've carried so many roles, responsibilities, expectations, even the quiet pressure to be everything for everyone. And now, something in you knows it's time to lay some of it down. Not because you're giving up, but because you're growing.

Letting go isn't weakness. It's wisdom. It takes strength to unclench your grip, to loosen your hold on things that once defined you. It takes courage to admit that some chapters have run their course. That you've outgrown certain versions of yourself.

This isn't about abandoning what you've built—it's about honoring it by making space for what's next.

Yes, there may be grief. There may be days when you miss the clarity of your old identity, the validation that came with your title, the rhythm of being needed. That's normal. You're human. And your feelings are sacred. You can hold pride and sadness in the same breath. You can honor what was while welcoming what's becoming.

Letting go is not losing yourself—it's meeting yourself again. In your fullness. In your quiet power. In your truth.

So give yourself permission to grieve, to rest, to breathe. Let the old fall away gently. You don't need to rush into the new.

You are not empty. You are spacious. And that space is holy.

With tenderness and truth,

Your Sister Who's Been There Too

7

Defining What Fulfillment Means to You

"We attract our highest and best good when we are in flow, not by forcing outcomes, but by holding clear vision and trusting the unfolding."

Success and Satisfaction

When you've spent most of your adult life measuring success by productivity, income, or achievement, the idea of fulfillment can feel abstract. But fulfillment isn't a luxury. It's a necessity. It's the sense that your life matters, that your time is meaningful, that what you do, and who you are, have value.

In retirement, many women discover that they've been chasing someone else's definition of success. It's only when we slow down that we realize: the things we thought would bring us joy (titles, accolades, material things) often leave us longing for something deeper.

Money Can't Buy Meaning

Let's be clear: financial stability is essential. We need to feel secure in our ability to care for ourselves and support the life we envision. However, we also need to recognize a more profound truth: money alone can never provide meaning or purpose.

True satisfaction comes from within, not from external validation. You could have all the material comforts in the world and still feel empty if your daily life lacks connection, creativity, or impact.

I've met women who seemed to "have it all" on the outside but privately told me, "I don't know who I am anymore." Fulfillment isn't about how things look. It's about how they feel.

Living Into Your Passions

Passion isn't just something for the young or the lucky. It's the fire within you that says, *This matters.* It's what makes you feel alive. Too often, we separate passion from practicality. We think *that's a hobby, not a calling.* But what if your greatest gift to the world is the thing that lights you up?

Have you ever wondered if there might be more to it all? What if you could wake up every morning knowing that you could do something you love while at the same time making a meaningful contribution to others?

The truth is that when we do the things we love, we show up in the world in a different way. We are joyful. That alone gives us the ability to transform others' lives. Our purpose is deeply intertwined with our passions.

Our passions are the things that make us joyful, irritated, angry, despondent, and blissful. When the work we do is something that we are passionate about, work—rather than being laborious—becomes play.

Purpose and the Road Less Traveled

We often find our purpose in the road less traveled. Most of us spend our lives trying to walk in the paths of others. We want what someone else has—their charisma, their status, their security. But when we're so focused on other people's journeys, we lose the ability to be present in our own lives.

It is in being present in our current circumstances that we find purpose. Purpose isn't usually revealed in one grand moment. It unfolds, like connecting dots in a picture. The process of discovering purpose is gradual, minute by minute, day by day.

Just when we think we've figured it out, life surprises us with a new facet of who we're meant to be.

Our families may have told us that following our passions was selfish or impractical. But some of the greatest contributions to the world come from unbridled passion allowed to run its course.
Paradoxically, the things that give us joy can also be our big "why." Joseph Campbell called it "following your bliss." When you follow what makes you come alive, you connect to a larger purpose and offer a unique contribution.

Our definitions of success shift over time, and that's not a flaw—it's growth.

> "In retirement, we have the chance to redefine success on our own terms, not society's."

—Shonda Rhimes

* * *

Soul-Aligned Living: A Return to What's True

As we move beyond the roles we've held, the titles we've carried, and the structures that once shaped our daily lives, we begin to ask deeper questions–not just about what we do, but about who we are and how we want to live.

Soul-aligned living is the courageous choice to live in integrity with your deepest truth. It's about letting your values, desires, and spiritual understanding—not external expectations — lead the way. It's not about abandoning responsibility or dismissing logic. It's about trusting that your soul carries wisdom that your resume never could.

This kind of living requires you to slow down. To listen inward. To question not only what you're doing, but why. It's a practice of alignment—of noticing where your inner life and outer choices are out of sync, and gently bringing them back into harmony.

For women of color in transition, soul-aligned living is particularly powerful. We've spent decades over-functioning, over-delivering, and navigating spaces that rarely reflected our whole selves. Now, we have a sacred invitation: to choose differently. To build lives that nourish, not deplete. To center joy, not just duty.

To say yes to what lights us up and no to what drains our spirit.

Returning to the Rhythm of Who You Are

Soul-aligned living is more than a concept–it's a remembering. It's the process of coming home to yourself after years, maybe decades, of centering everyone and everything else.

As women of color, especially those who have led, created, built, and held space for others, it can be easy to lose sight of the quiet truths of who we are beneath all the doing.

This is not about being perfect. It's about being honest. It's about letting your inner wisdom set the pace of your life — and honoring it as sacred.

After leaving the structured world of leadership and work, many of us find ourselves asking: What matters now? What feels real? What is calling to me, not from expectation, but from essence? These are not easy questions. But they are the right ones.

Soul-aligned living is about...

- *Releasing what no longer fits–even if it once did.*
- *Listening to your body, your spirit, your intuition.*
- *Allowing joy, rest, and peace to guide your choices.*

Choosing relationships, rhythms, and responsibilities that feel life-giving, not life-depleting.

This is not self-indulgence. This is stewardship. Of your energy. Of your gifts. Of your one, sacred life.

A Way of Being, Not a To-Do List

Soul-aligned living is not a set of habits or hacks. It's a way of being. It's a return to your inner compass–one that has always been there, waiting to be heard beneath the noise. It doesn't require perfection. It requires presence.

You don't need anyone's permission to live this way. Not anymore.

This is your moment to come home to yourself. To live guided by what's real. To build a life not just of productivity or legacy, but of meaning, resonance, and deep internal peace.

Because fulfillment isn't something you find out there, it's something you align with in here.

What Soul-Aligned Living Looks Like in Practice

You've already been living in alignment in pieces—now you get to live in it fully. Here's what it can look like:

- **Choosing joy over obligation.** No longer saying yes because you "should," but because you want to.
- **Creating slow mornings.** Sacred rituals that open your day with peace, not pressure.
- Building your week around rest. Scheduling restoration before productivity.
- **Letting go of identities that were rooted in survival.** Creating new ones rooted in wholeness.
- **Following your curiosity.** Letting inspiration, not guilt, lead you.
- **Trusting divine timing.** Surrendering control in favor of flow.

You don't need to "retire" into a version of yourself that feels flat or empty. You get to rise into your realest self, the one that was always there, just waiting for space to breathe.

Final Thought

There is nothing more powerful than a woman who remembers who she is. Who aligns her outer life with her inner knowing. Who lives not from fear or habit, but from purpose and presence.

This season of your life is not about reinvention—it's about reclamation.

Live soul-first.

* * *

Practicing Fulfillment Daily

Fulfillment isn't a far-off goal—it's something we can nurture each day. One small decision, one aligned action, one sacred moment at a time.

Ask yourself:

- What makes me feel vibrant?
- What gives me a sense of peace?
- What sparks my curiosity?
- When do I feel most like myself?

Once you start noticing what brings you joy and energy, you can build a life that includes more of it. Fulfillment is not an abstract ideal—it's a practice. A rhythm. A way of being that we come back to again and again.

You might:

- Schedule weekly time for your creative passions
- Have regular check-ins with yourself or a trusted friend
- Reflect monthly on what brought you fulfillment—and what didn't

These practices become a compass, gently steering you toward a life of meaning.

A Spiritual Perspective on Fulfillment

I had a dream once where I heard the words, "How do you create a revolution? One person at a time."

Many of the problems we face today are dis-eases of the spirit that manifest in various ways. By addressing both the physical and spiritual aspects of well-being, we find true healing and purpose.

That's become my mission—I'm a revolutionary at heart, working to transform lives by helping people connect with their own spiritual nature and overall well-being.

Your Fulfillment, Your Legacy

Fulfillment and legacy are not separate ideas. Your fulfillment now lays the groundwork for the legacy you leave. When you live with passion, intention, and authenticity, you inspire others to do the same. That ripple effect becomes part of the imprint you leave on the world.

Let your fulfillment be a living legacy—one that can be felt, witnessed, and remembered in every word you speak and every space you enter.

Journaling Prompt: Discovering Your Fulfillment

Write about a time in your life when you felt deeply fulfilled. What were you doing? Who were you with? What values were you honoring?

Now reflect:

- What passions have you put on hold?
- What activities or interests energize you?
- What impact do you want to have in the next phase of your life?
- What would it look like to live fully into your purpose?

You do not have to chase your purpose. It never left you. Engage in deeper conversations with yourself. What you love and what you despise can help reveal your path.

Fulfillment is not a finish line. It's a way of being. Let this chapter be your invitation to choose meaning over metrics, passion over pressure, and presence over perfection.

You are the author of this new story, and fulfillment is the theme that will carry you forward.

8

Spotlight: What I Wish I Knew

If I could sit with my younger self—the one who was just starting to feel the edges of transition—I'd hold her hands, look her in the eyes, and say:

You don't have to have it all figured out.

I know how much pressure you feel to be strong. To make the next move look graceful, wise, and strategic. You've spent years leading, solving, and showing up—and now that everything is shifting, you think you have to manage this perfectly too.

But you don't. And here's what I wish I knew back then:

You Are Allowed to Mourn and Celebrate at the Same Time

No one tells you how complex this season can be. One moment you're grieving the loss of identity, structure, or status—and the next, you feel free and full of possibility. It's confusing.

I wish I'd known that joy and sorrow can sit side by side. That letting go of one role doesn't mean abandoning your power. That change doesn't always feel like clarity, but it can still be right.

Your Worth Is Not Tied to Your Work

I wish I'd learned this earlier: You are worthy, full stop. Not because of what you do or how well you lead or how many people need you, but because of who you are.

It's easy to feel invisible when the accolades stop, when people stop asking for your input, when the emails and invitations slow down. But you are not your inbox. You are not your job title. You are a whole person with infinite value.

Your Dreams Are Still Alive—and Still Possible

Some dreams take their time. Others are waiting for you to be ready, not in skill, but in soul. I wish I hadn't pushed those dreams to the back burner for so long. I wish I'd made room for creativity, play, and curiosity. Not just productivity.

It's not too late. Your dreams didn't expire. They're just waiting for you to believe in them again.

Rest Is Not a Reward—It's a Right

You do not have to earn your rest.

You do not have to explain your need for stillness.

I wish I had treated rest as a sacred rhythm instead of a stolen moment. Rest is where you hear yourself again. Rest is where the soul unclenches. It's not the opposite of impact—it's the foundation of it.

Community Will Look Different—And That's Okay

When you leave behind a workplace, a role, or even a way of being, your circle may shift. Some people will fall away. Others will rise into your life in new ways.

I wish I'd known not to panic when I felt alone at first. The people who are meant for your next chapter will show up. And so will the ones who see you fully, beyond your résumé, beyond your roles.

You Can Lead From a Different Place Now

Leadership doesn't disappear when you step back. It evolves. You get to influence from a place of wholeness now. Without burnout. Without needing the spotlight. You get to speak when you want to, not because you have to.

Your impact might be quieter now, but it might also be deeper.

You Deserve Joy Without Explanation

You don't need to explain why you want to travel, paint, nap, laugh, write, or just sit and do nothing for a while. That's not frivolous—that's freedom.

Joy is not a detour. It's the destination.

It's Okay to Start Over

It's okay not to know what's next.

It's okay to try something new and decide it's not for you.

It's okay to begin again, at any age, for any reason.

You are not behind. You are not lost. You are unfolding.

If any of this sounds like it might be true for you now, let it in. You don't need to go back and do it differently. You simply get to do it differently *now*.

What I wish I knew then... I know now.

And I'm passing it on to you.

9

Exploring New Avenues for Impact

"When we live from joy and not duty, our passions become our offering. This is the path of legacy—work that feeds others while feeding you too."

This Is Not the End—It's a New Beginning

For women of color transitioning out of organizational leadership, retirement doesn't mean disappearing—it means reemerging. You are not retiring from purpose. You are stepping into a new era where your voice, your wisdom, and your leadership can thrive in more authentic, impactful ways.

Think of this as a creative phase of your life—one where you get to blend experience, passion, and vision to make the kind of difference that aligns with your soul. The world needs what you know and who you are. Now, more than ever.

Redefining Contribution

Many women find that their deepest contributions come after retirement. It's no longer about climbing the ladder or meeting someone else's goals—it's about using your gifts where they're most needed. You've already done the proving. Now you get to do the giving—from a place of abundance.

Here are a few pathways women are exploring:

- **Mentorship and Empowerment:** Guiding younger professionals, especially women of color, through the challenges of leadership, identity, and balance.
- **Board Leadership:** Bringing diverse perspectives into nonprofit, education, and corporate boardrooms.
- **Social Entrepreneurship:** Launching mission-driven ventures that address community needs.
- **Philanthropy and Advocacy:** Supporting causes you care about—not just with money, but with strategy and visibility.
- **Writing and Speaking:** Sharing your story to shift narratives and shape the next generation of leadership.
- **Teaching and Research:** Joining community colleges, seminar series, or even auditing courses to expand your impact and knowledge.

One of the most beautiful truths of this stage is that your impact doesn't have to be loud or grand to be meaningful. A heartfelt conversation, a small community program, a story shared at the right time—these are all seeds of change.

What Legacy Work Really Means

Legacy isn't just about what you leave behind—it's about how you live now. Each choice, each connection, each project can be part of the imprint you leave on the world.

Retirement gives you time to ask:

- What matters most to me?
- Who do I want to serve?
- What kind of example do I want to set for the next generation?

Legacy work doesn't always require funding or a formal structure. It might be the intentional ways you show up for your family. It could be creating family archives or oral histories. It might be mentoring a neighbor's child, advocating for local policy changes, or planting a community garden.

Stories of Modern-Day Trailblazers

- **Dr. Johnnetta Cole**, the first African American woman president of Spelman College, has spent her retirement advocating for diversity in museums and cultural institutions.
- **Ursula Burns**, former CEO of Xerox, now focuses on STEM education for underrepresented youth.
- **Indra Nooyi**, former CEO of PepsiCo, serves on multiple boards and is a global advocate for sustainable leadership and caregiving policies.
- **Cynthia**, a former HR executive, started a spiritual wellness retreat center for midlife women of color. "I wanted to create the space I never had," she says. "A place where we could rest and be restored."

They didn't step back—they stepped forward in new ways. So can you.

Owning Your Expertise and Influence

Too often, we minimize our experience because it doesn't look like what's currently trending. But your voice and your story matter precisely *because* they carry lived wisdom.

This is your time to own:

- Your expertise
- Your ability to lead, influence, and inspire
- The value of what you've built—even if it was behind the scenes

Whether you're helping a nonprofit structure its HR policies, mentoring a startup founder, or offering guidance to a local church board, your expertise is currency—and you get to decide how it's spent.

* * *

Translating Skills into Legacy Work

After years of working in leadership roles--navigating systems, solving problems, mentoring teams--you've cultivated a toolkit of skills that is both powerful and priceless.

But as you move into a new chapter of life, you may be wondering: What do I do with all this wisdom now?

The beautiful truth is this: your professional skills are not lost. They are ripe for reinvention. They don't need to be boxed into retirement--they can be transformed into living legacy work that nourishes both you and your community.

Let's explore how.

From Expertise to Empowerment

The first step in this transformation is recognizing that your knowledge still has value--even outside formal titles or institutions. Legacy work starts when you take what you know and use it to uplift, educate, or inspire others.

That might mean:

- *Offering pro bono strategic support to a grassroots organization*
- *Creating a workshop for young women entering your former field*
- *Writing or speaking publicly about what you've learned*
- *Consulting or mentoring on a part-time basis, with complete freedom over your schedule*
- *Your influence no longer has to be tied to output. It can be measured by the impact you make on someone else's life.*

You are now in a position to be a guide, a mirror, a seed-planter. That is a powerful role.

Skill Mapping: What You Already Have

Many women underestimate their transferable talents. They think, I'm not sure what I can offer now, because their skills were always used in specific contexts. But legacy work is about re-imagining context, not discarding capacity.

Here's how to begin a skill inventory:

- **Strategic Thinking** → Community leadership, advisory boards, or nonprofit planning
- **Team Development** → Coaching or mentoring emerging leaders
- **Communication Skills** → Public speaking, blogging, writing op-eds, or curriculum
- **Project Management** → Helping local initiatives grow, planning services, or cultural events
- **Financial Literacy** → Teaching financial independence courses to underserved communities
- **Conflict Resolution** → Facilitating inter-generational conversations or healing circles

These are not just "hard skills." They are human skills. They are community-building skills.

They are legacy-building tools.

Creative Applications: Legacy in Action

Let's bring this idea down to earth with a few real-world examples:

Lorna, *a retired operations executive, now hosts quarterly planning retreats for women-owned businesses in her community. She brings her corporate structure knowledge to soulful, heart-led spaces.*

Tasha, *once a school principal, now records short audio messages on parenting, purpose, and policy. She shares them through WhatsApp groups with mothers in her church and family network.*

Carmen, *a financial analyst, now hosts informal kitchen table money talks for women in her neighborhood. She teaches wealth-building* *strategies in language that feels accessible, respectful, and culturally relevant.*

These women didn't reinvent themselves from scratch. They took what they already knew and let it evolve into something purpose-driven and nourishing.

And you can too.

Ask Yourself: What Legacy Feels Like

To translate your skills into legacy, you must first connect with what legacy means to you. It doesn't have to be grand. It doesn't have to go viral. It just has to feel true.

Ask:

- *What do I want to pass on?*
- *Who do I feel called to support or invest in?*
- *What am I tired of holding—and what am I excited to give?*
- *What unmet needs does my community have?*

Legacy work isn't always glamorous. Often, it's quiet. A conversation. A resource. A story passed down. A practice shared. It is how wisdom moves from generation to generation.

Legacy That Nourishes You Too

Here's the thing: your legacy work should feed you, too. It should feel joyful, affirming, purposeful, not just dutiful.

This might mean:

- *Choosing how and when you share your time and energy*
- *Charging a fair fee for your time, or offering it freely, on your terms*
- *Partnering with younger women to share the load and create sustainability*
- *Setting boundaries so that your giving doesn't drain you*

When your legacy is built from love, not pressure, it becomes sustainable. It becomes an extension of your wholeness, not a continuation of over-functioning.

True legacy doesn't come from duty—it comes from desire, from what lights you up.

Returning to the Rhythm of Who You Are

Soul-aligned living is more than a concept—it's a remembering. It's the process of coming home to yourself after years, maybe decades, of centering everyone and everything else.

As women of color, especially those who have led, created, built, and held space for others, it can be easy to lose sight of the quiet truths of who we are beneath all the doing.

This is not about being perfect. It's about being honest. It's about letting your inner wisdom set the pace of your life and honoring it as sacred.

After leaving the structured world of leadership and work, many of us find ourselves asking: What matters now? What feels real? What is calling to me, not from expectation, but from essence? These are not easy questions. But they are the right ones.

> "Don't ask yourself what the world needs. Ask yourself what makes you come alive and then go do that."
> –Howard Thurman

Journaling Prompts: Skills into Legacy

Use these questions to reflect or write:

- What are three skills I'm proud of mastering in my career?
- How can I apply these skills beyond a traditional workplace?
- Who is someone in my life who could benefit from what I've learned?
- What would a "legacy project" look like if it centered joy, not just impact?

Let your answers come slowly. They may arrive as ideas, images, conversations, or even resistance.

* * *

Your Professional Skills Still Matter

Don't underestimate the power of your career experience. The same skills that made you successful in leadership—strategic thinking, communication, conflict resolution, vision—are gold in community organizations, policy work, and entrepreneurship.

You don't have to start over. You get to start *differently*. Take stock of your gifts:

- What are you naturally good at?

- What do people seek you out for?
- How would you like to utilize those gifts now?

As you begin to imagine how your gifts can serve the world in new ways, remember: this season is not about starting over. It's about stepping forward with freedom, clarity, and heart.

> *"Innovation and entrepreneurship are not about the money, but about the independence, making a difference, and changing the world."*
> —Kiran Mazumdar-Shaw, Founder, Biocon Limited.

You have nothing to prove. But you have so much to give. Let your next offering reflect your authentic truth, not the expectations of the world.

Sometimes, your next step isn't starting something new—it's reimagining what you already know how to do. A coach becomes a spiritual guide. A teacher becomes a storyteller. A strategist becomes a nonprofit founder.

Technology, Creativity, and Lifelong Learning

Many women are using technology to expand their reach, starting online businesses, launching podcasts, leading virtual courses, or even creating digital archives of family or cultural history. Technology is no longer just for the young—it's for the curious.

Others are diving into creative pursuits, such as painting, dancing, storytelling, and photography. These aren't just hobbies—they're tools for transformation. They reconnect us with our intuition, open up new forms of expression, and allow us to contribute beauty to the world.

And then there's learning. So many of us left things on the back burner—interests we shelved for survival's sake. Now's the time to go back to school, take a class, learn a language, and explore a new philosophy. Lifelong learning keeps your spirit alive.

Community as a Platform for Purpose

Connection is key. Retirement can be isolating if your social life was tied to your work. But it can also be liberating—an opportunity to cultivate relationships that nourish your soul.

Find or build communities that reflect your values:

- Inter-generational circles
- Leadership forums
- Cultural organizations
- Wellness and spirituality groups

In these communities, you don't have to explain your worth—it's already understood. You can simply be. You can share wisdom, receive support, and explore your impact without performance or pretense.

One of the women in my circle once said, "I spent 30 years managing teams. Now I manage my joy." Her calendar is full—not with meetings, but with meaning. Volunteering. Storytelling. Gardening. Hosting meals for young women who remind her of who she used to be.

Navigating the Fear of Visibility or Starting Over

Sometimes, we shrink from impact because we think we're too old, too late, too tired. Let me gently challenge that: it is never too late to be powerful. It is never too late to show up for yourself or others.

You may not want the spotlight, but that doesn't mean you can't be a light. Impact isn't always public. It's the unseen kindness, the legacy of courage, the quiet transformation of a family or community because you chose to step forward.

Don't let fear of imperfection keep you from starting. You don't need a perfect plan—just a clear intention. What matters is that you begin.

As we begin to explore what lasting impact looks like in this new season, we must also redefine what responsibility means. Legacy is not about shouldering more weight—it's about offering what's truest in us with humility and grace.

> "Humility is not a matter of self-effacement and self-negation but of being open always to new ways of being responsible."
> —Ada María Isasi-Díaz, Mujerista theologian

This kind of humility is not a matter of smallness. It is expansion. It is alignment. It is a contribution that flows from the soul, not status.

Journaling Prompt: Mapping Your Impact

Reflect on your journey:

- What kinds of impact have brought you the most joy?
- Who do you feel called to serve or uplift?
- What unmet need or opportunity keeps coming to mind?
- What's one bold step you can take in that direction?

Create a list of five ways you could contribute—big or small. Circle the one that lights you up. Then, do one small thing toward it this week.

Final Thoughts

Let your next chapter be as purposeful as your last—but infinitely more free. You are not finished. You are just beginning to rise in a new way. With your experience, your heart, and your voice, you have everything you need to make this next season your most impactful one yet.

You are not retiring—you are re-imagining. This is your invitation to build a legacy rooted in love, alignment, and bold creativity. Let the work begin.

10

Financial Freedom: Beyond Mindset

"Once we tap into the larger stream, money becomes secondary. What we need arrives—not when we want it, but when we're truly ready."

The Foundation Is Not the House

Financial planning is often seen as the cornerstone of retirement. It's necessary—like the foundation of a house. But here's the truth: the foundation is not the house. The house is where you live. The house is your joy, your peace, your contribution, your fulfillment.

Financial freedom isn't just about money. It's about choices. It's about being able to say yes to the things that matter and no to the things that don't. It's about designing a life that aligns with your values, not just your budget.

Beyond the Numbers

We've been taught to define wealth in purely material terms. Net worth, retirement savings, assets and liabilities. But wealth, in its original sense, meant well-being. It's time we return to that definition.

Genuine wealth includes:

- Our cultural wisdom and lived experiences
- The strength of our relationships and communities
- Our ability to empower others
- The legacy we build
- The values we uphold

There's a paradox we see again and again: people with financial abundance who live in fear and scarcity. And others with modest means who live joyfully, making deep impacts in their communities. The difference is not in the bank account—it's in the orientation toward wealth.

The Power of Stewardship

Wealth isn't about having unlimited resources—it's about how we steward what we have. As women of color, we've often been stewards out of necessity. We've made magic out of limited budgets. We've stretched dollars and created comfort, stability, and celebration where others saw lack.

Financial freedom asks us to take that wisdom and pair it with clarity and intention. It's about:

- Knowing what you need and what you don't

- Understanding your priorities
- Honoring your dreams without apology

> *"True alignment happens when we clear the energetic and emotional blocks tied to money. Once we release old stories of scarcity and survival, we begin to attract and manage resources with power and grace."*

A Life Plan Over a Financial Plan

Money is a tool, not the goal. What's more powerful than a financial plan? A life plan. One that asks:

- How do I want to live?
- What will bring me joy?
- What legacy do I want to create?
- How do I want to feel every day?

A sound financial plan supports this vision. But it should never define it. Your life plan is the blueprint—the vision. Your finances? They're the scaffolding that helps build the dream.

Freedom from Financial Fear

One of the most liberating realizations is that financial security is not something money can ever truly provide. Security isn't based on external conditions. It comes from our orientation to the world, our trust in ourselves, and our sense of divine connection. When we live in alignment with our values, the universe responds in kind.

> *"Security cannot come from or be based on financial things. Money is energy and therefore has an impetus to flow, transform and change. If we are looking to money (or any external thing) for security, we will always be left wanting."*

Security begins with how we see ourselves. It flows from confidence, clarity, and a spiritual knowing that we are cared for and provided for, even in times of uncertainty.

Strategies That Honor the Whole You

Women of color face unique financial realities—wage gaps, career interruptions, caregiving responsibilities. That's why we need strategies that are both practical and personal:

- **Flexible Income Streams**: Consulting, part-time work, or entrepreneurship that honors your time and purpose.
- **Smart Health Planning**: Prioritize preventative care and budget for wellness, understanding health disparities.
- **Legacy Planning**: Not just financial inheritance, but cultural, spiritual, and wisdom-based legacies.
- **Personal Development Funds**: Budget for learning, travel, creative pursuits, or starting a venture.
- **Inter-generational Wealth-Building**: Teaching financial literacy, mentoring young adults, co-investing in community projects.

Financial freedom also means teaching others. For many, retirement becomes a time to pass on what they've learned through workshops, family meetings, or financial coaching within their communities.

Experiences Over Stuff

More and more, women of color are choosing meaningful experiences over material goods. This shift is not just cultural—it's deeply personal. Many are investing in travel, spiritual retreats, creative workshops, and knowledge-sharing gatherings. The value lies in memory, growth, and connection.

Imagine budgeting not for a bigger car but for a healing retreat in Sedona. Not for designer clothes, but for an artist residency. Not for status, but for self-expression.

These are not luxuries. They are investments in your soul.

Spiritual Wealth and Money as Energy

Money is more than currency—it's energy. It reflects our beliefs, fears, and dreams. When we change our relationship with money, we change our relationship with power.

Spiritual wealth asks:

- Are you in right relationship with your resources?
- Do you trust yourself to make aligned financial choices?
- Are you able to receive without guilt and give without depletion?

These questions help us reframe abundance—not as excess, but as flow. As alignment. As trust.

When you can sit with what is, rather than constantly wishing for more or less, you step into a profound space of financial alignment. At the end of the day we all want to be free from worry... and the revelation is that we can choose that at any moment.

Creating Balance

Balance in finances, like in life, doesn't mean stasis—it means flow. Sometimes you save. Sometimes you invest. Sometimes you give. The key is awareness. Intention. Balance allows for joy without fear, generosity without guilt, planning without obsession.

This also includes ethical investing—putting your money into companies or projects that align with your values, such as sustainable energy, women-owned businesses, or initiatives that support marginalized communities.

Journaling Prompt: Designing Your Abundant Life

1. What does financial freedom mean to you today?
2. What stories about money are you ready to release?
3. What does an abundant life look and feel like in this season?
4. What practical steps can you take to align your money with your values?
5. What legacy of wealth—material, emotional, and spiritual—do you want to leave?

Final Thoughts

Your worth is not your wallet. Your wealth is not your worry. Your power lies in your ability to align your resources with your values and vision.

Financial freedom isn't the end goal. It's the beginning of a life built with clarity, courage, and care. As you continue this journey, know that you are not here to simply survive—you are here to thrive, give, enjoy, and leave something lasting.

This chapter isn't about spreadsheets—it's about sovereignty. Reclaim it. Define it. Live it—on your terms.

11

Letter to My Sister

To the Sister Dreaming Again

"There is still time. There is still room. Your dreams are not too late. They are right on time."

Dear Sister,

I see that flicker in your eyes—the one you almost forgot was there.

You're dreaming again. Not out loud, maybe not even boldly yet, but something in you is stirring. A vision. A longing. A whisper that says, *there's more for me.*

And I want you to know: it's not too late.

Your dreams are not frivolous. They are sacred. They are echoes of who you've always been—buried under obligation, softened by sacrifice, shaped by survival. But they never left. They've just been waiting for you to return.

Let go of the idea that dreaming is only for the young. You have the depth, the wisdom, and the perspective to dream better now. Freer. Truer. Wiser.

This time, you don't need to ask for permission. You don't need to justify the desire. You don't have to monetize it or prove its worth. Your joy is reason enough.

Whether your dream is to start something new or simply to feel more alive in your everyday life, let it bloom. Let it be awkward, messy, slow. Let it unfold on its own time.

And please, don't dream small just because it feels safer. You've already done brave things. You can do this, too.

Your dreams are not a return to who you were. They are a bold declaration of who you're becoming.

Dream on, Sister. The world still needs your light.

With wonder and warmth,

Your Sister Who Believes in You

III

Building Community & Legacy

You were never meant to walk this journey alone. Building community now is about connection rooted in shared values, support, and joy. It's time to surround yourself with people who see you, uplift you, and walk beside you as you grow into this next chapter, together.

12

Sisterhood & Support: The Power of Connection

"It's not about being rescued. It's about being seen, heard, and held by those who help you remember who you are."

You Don't Have to Do This Alone

For many of us, career success meant forging ahead—even when we were the only woman of color in the room. We had to be strong, composed, and often silent about the challenges we faced. We carried the expectations of our families and communities, sometimes at significant personal cost.

But in this new chapter, you get to let that go. You get to rest. And you get to connect with others, with yourself, and with something greater than your individual journey.

This is the time to lean into sisterhood, to surround yourself with women who see you, support you, and celebrate your evolution. This isn't about networking—it's about soul connection. It's about creating a circle of wisdom, care, and power.

The Healing Power of Community

Community is more than companionship—it's a source of healing. When we gather in circles, we bear witness to each other's journeys. We remind each other of our brilliance. We hold space for transformation.

As women of color, our experiences are unique, and so are our wounds. We've often had to code-switch, suppress parts of ourselves, and carry the emotional weight of being the "only." Finding a community where we can show up fully and be affirmed is not just restorative—it's revolutionary.

Supportive community brings:

- Emotional safety and mutual respect
- Cultural understanding without explanation
- Intergenerational wisdom-sharing
- Space to grieve, dream, and rebuild

When we find women who truly "get it," we begin to relax. We begin to open. We begin to heal.

Building Your Circle of Support

Your new season deserves new support. This might include:

- **Peer Circles:** A small group of women navigating similar transitions.
- **Mentorship Networks:** Where you are both mentor and mentee.
- **Spiritual Communities:** Grounding spaces that nourish your soul.
- **Creative Collaboratives:** Groups where expression is encouraged and affirmed.

Start by asking:

- Who energizes me?
- Who listens deeply?
- Who challenges me with love?
- Who helps me stay true to my values?

You don't need dozens of people. Even two or three strong, intentional relationships can provide a robust support system.

The Value of Intergenerational Wisdom

One of the most enriching aspects of this chapter is the opportunity to connect across generations. Younger women need your insight. Elders offer perspective. When we gather, we bridge gaps, heal ancestral wounds, and build collective strength.

Host intergenerational dialogues. Mentor a rising leader. Ask an elder about her journey. Record family stories. These exchanges not only uplift others—they ground and nourish you.

As one woman put it, "I thought I was too old to mentor. But what I found was that I needed them just as much as they needed me."

Safe Spaces for Truth-Telling

In community, we can tell the truth. About our fears. Our losses. Our joys. Our longings. We don't have to perform. We don't have to pretend. We can just be.

Create spaces for vulnerability:

- Story circles or healing salons
- Journaling groups
- Wellness retreats
- Guided discussions on aging, identity, and purpose

The truth-telling that happens in sacred circles is transformative. It gives us permission to live more freely, love more deeply, and speak more boldly.

Sisterhood in Action: Creating Collective Impact

Community is not just about receiving—it's about creating together. Women of color are forming powerful collectives in retirement that:

- Launch nonprofits
- Mentor youth
- Create economic cooperatives
- Build cultural and spiritual wellness hubs

These efforts don't require massive infrastructure. They begin with a conversation. A shared dream. A willingness to build something meaningful together.

Letting Go of Lone Wolf Syndrome

In leadership, we often had to "go it alone." We wore self-reliance as armor. But now, we get to take off the armor. We get to ask for help. We get to say, "I don't know."

Lone wolf syndrome may have served you once, but it will not sustain you now. True freedom is knowing you're supported. That you can lean back and someone will catch you.

Finding Your People

If you're wondering where to find your people, start by exploring spaces where your values are reflected. Look for:

- Cultural institutions and affinity groups
- Online communities for women of color in midlife
- Local wellness or social justice initiatives
- Creative or spiritual circles

And remember—you can also *create* the community you crave. If it doesn't exist, build it. Invite two women over for tea and start there.

Exploring Digital Sisterhood

Technology has expanded the ways we connect. You can now find support, healing, and friendship with women across the country or even the globe.

Platforms like Zoom, Mighty Networks, Facebook Groups, and Clubhouse have made it easier to:

- Host virtual sister circles
- Join interest-based communities (from wellness to entrepreneurship)
- Attend online retreats, book clubs, and healing spaces

Don't underestimate the power of a virtual connection. Many lifelong bonds now begin with a DM or a shared post. Digital sisterhood can be just as nourishing as in-person connection when it's built on mutual respect and intention.

Facilitating a Circle: A Simple Guide

Want to build your sister circle but not sure where to start? Please keep it simple. Here's a structure:

1. **Set an intention** – Make it clear that the circle is a space for honesty, support, and joy.
2. **Create a rhythm** – Monthly or biweekly gatherings work well.
3. **Offer a theme** – Each session could explore identity, self-care, purpose, creativity, or aging.
4. **Open with grounding** – A poem, meditation, or breathwork helps center the group.
5. **Encourage sharing** – Allow everyone a chance to speak and be witnessed.
6. **Close with gratitude** – End by reflecting on what was gained.

Over time, your circle may grow, deepen, and become one of your most treasured sources of support.

Stories of Connection and Belonging

Marisol, a retired attorney, began hosting Sunday brunches for Black and Latina women in her neighborhood. What started as a social gathering evolved into a space for vision boarding, financial planning, and soulful conversations.

Cynthia, a former executive, co-founded a storytelling circle for women of color to share their life journeys. "It's the first time I felt seen for all of who I am," she said.

Janelle, an artist, started a monthly potluck that became an intergenerational sanctuary of joy, food, and wisdom-sharing. "We laugh, we cry, and we heal together."

Their stories are not extraordinary—they're examples of what's possible when we prioritize connection.

How Sisterhood Sustains Us

Sisterhood isn't a buzzword—it's a lifeline. When the road feels uncertain, it's the call from a friend that reminds you of your power. It's the shared laughter that lifts your spirit. It's the knowing glance across a room that says, "I've got you."

In sisterhood, we:

- Share wisdom, not judgment
- Witness one another's growth
- Offer grace, not comparison
- Celebrate each other's wins

Sisterhood reminds us we're never alone in the journey. It reminds us of our resilience. Our joy. Our collective strength.

Journaling Prompt: Cultivating Connection

- Who are the women in your life who truly see and support you?
- What kinds of community do you crave?
- Where can you offer support or mentorship?
- What is one step you can take this week to nurture sisterhood?
- What would your ideal circle of support look like—and how can you begin to create it?

Final Thoughts

This next season is not meant to be walked alone. It is meant to be danced, marched, and meandered in the company of women who hold your story with reverence.

Build the circle. Join the table. Share your voice. And when you feel weary, let sisterhood carry you.

Because together, we are unstoppable. We rise stronger when we rise together.

Mutual care is not just helpful—it's essential for our collective thriving.

"The only way to survive is by taking care of one another."
—Grace Lee Boggs, Activist

13

Letter to My Sister

To the Sister Who Feels Alone

"You are not forgotten. You are not invisible. You are not alone. We're out here, too—ready to walk with you."

Dear Sister,

If you're feeling a little invisible right now, a little disconnected, I want you to know—I see you. I feel you. I've been there too.

Transitions can be lonely. Especially when you've spent years surrounded by people, titles, meetings, responsibilities. And now? The phone's not ringing as much. The calendar's not full. The pace has changed—and so has your place in it all.

It's okay to feel unmoored. It's okay to miss the rhythm of being needed, the clarity of your role. But hear me when I say this: your value did not leave with your title. Your voice is still powerful. Your presence still matters. You are not forgotten.

Sometimes, we just need someone to remind us that we still belong.

Community may look different now. It may be quieter, deeper, more intentional. You might have to seek it—or build it yourself. But it's there. We are out here. Women who know the sacredness of your story, who understand your journey, who long to walk with you too.

You don't have to do this alone. You were never meant to.

Reach out, even if your voice shakes. Send the text. Join the circle. Speak your truth in a room where someone else is silently waiting to hear it.

Because your story could be the lifeline someone else is hoping for.

You are seen. You are loved. And you are absolutely not alone.

With solidarity and open arms,

Your Sister in the Circle

14

Leaving a Legacy Beyond Work

*"Our legacy is more than what we leave behind. It's who we become—
and how generously we share that becoming while we're still here*

What Will You Leave Behind?

We often think of legacy as something that happens after we're gone. But the truth is that we're building our legacy every day through the choices we make, the lives we touch, and the stories we share. As a woman of color transitioning into retirement, you are in a powerful position to shape what your legacy will look like—not someday, but now.

You've likely spent your career overcoming barriers, mentoring others, and modeling excellence. Now, it's time to turn inward and ask: *What do I want to be remembered for? What values do I want to pass on? What change do I still want to make in the world?*

Redefining Legacy for Ourselves

Legacy doesn't have to mean having a building named after you or a major foundation in your honor. It can be as simple and as profound as how you made people feel, the wisdom you shared, and the space you created for others to grow.

Legacy is:

- Sharing your lived experience so others don't have to learn the hard way
- Documenting family history and cultural traditions
- Starting a program that uplifts your community
- Showing younger women what it looks like to live and lead authentically
- Modeling grace and joy in the face of aging and change

Your legacy is not one grand gesture—it's the accumulation of your impact, day by day, decision by decision. Sometimes it's woven into your garden, your meals, your journal entries, your movement. Sometimes legacy shows up in the art of everyday life.

> "Art is doing. Art deals directly with life."
> —Ruth Asawa

It is evident in the way you care for your loved ones, in how you manage your time and energy, and in the presence you bring to any room. Creativity isn't separate from purpose—it is purpose, embodied. Let what you love to do become a part of what you leave behind.

An Invitation to Intentional Living

Now is the time to shift from achievement to alignment. From proving to preserving. From producing to passing it on. This is your invitation to live in such a way that your values echo beyond your presence.

Ask yourself:

- What kind of ancestor do I want to be?
- How can I make choices now that reflect who I truly am?
- Where can I plant seeds that will bloom long after I'm gone?
- How do I want people to remember my presence?

There is a season for everything, including the season to give differently.

> *"To every thing there is a season, and a time to every purpose under the heaven."*
> —*Ecclesiastes 3:1*

Sharing Your Story

Our stories are one of the most powerful legacies we can offer. For too long, the narratives about women of color have been told *for* us or *about* us, but not *by* us. Writing your story, speaking your truth, or recording your reflections ensures that your journey becomes a guidepost for others.

Consider:

- Writing a memoir, blog, or letters to future generations
- Recording oral histories with family members
- Hosting storytelling circles in your community
- Contributing to archives or cultural preservation projects
- Sharing faith journeys and spiritual revelations that sustained you

Your story holds power. It teaches. It heals. It leads. And perhaps most of all, it affirms our collective experience and shared humanity.

Mentorship as Legacy

Mentorship is one of the most impactful ways to pass on your legacy. Whether formally or informally, sharing your insights with emerging leaders can have a profound impact on their lives. You don't have to have all the answers—you need to be willing to share your journey.

As one retired executive put it: "I didn't realize how much I had to offer until a young woman asked me to help her prepare for a panel. That one conversation turned into a mentorship relationship that changed both of us."

Ways to mentor:

- Join formal mentorship programs for professionals
- Offer your expertise to nonprofits or community initiatives
- Host small salons or circles where women can learn from each other
- Start a legacy mentorship journal—a simple guide for navigating leadership, balance, and authenticity

Creative Legacy

Your legacy can also be expressed in a creative way. Retirement opens the door to explore art, music, writing, or craft—forms of expression that may have been sidelined during your career. Creative work can serve as a powerful expression of identity, culture, and contribution.

Start small:

- Paint a series of portraits inspired by your lineage
- Write a book of poetry or personal essays
- Design a workshop that combines your professional wisdom with spiritual insight
- Compose a family blessing or affirmation to pass on

The goal isn't perfection. Its presence. Let your creativity be a part of how you are remembered.

> *"...which causes me to wonder... what is beautiful that I make? What is elegant? What feeds the world?"*
> —Louise Erdrich

Building Inter-generational Bridges

Legacy also means investing in the generations that follow. Many retired women of color are:

- Hosting inter-generational retreats
- Starting scholarship funds
- Teaching traditional skills to their grandchildren
- Organizing cultural immersion trips to ancestral homelands

Ask your children and grandchildren what they want to learn from you. What would they like to know about your past? What advice do they hope you'll share? These simple questions can open the door to connection and wisdom-sharing that lasts for generations.

Advocacy and Systems Change

Your legacy can also be systemic. Many women are using their retirement years to:

- Advocate for equity in healthcare and retirement policies
- Run for local office
- Consult with organizations on DEI practices
- Develop programs that serve underserved populations

You have the lived experience, credibility, and time to influence real change. Don't underestimate the power of your voice, especially when paired with intention and clarity.

Coalition-Building and Collective Power

Legacy isn't only personal. It can also be collective. Consider:

- Partnering with other retired women to create a leadership circle
- Forming a fund or grant to support creative projects by women of color
- Hosting summits, salons, or book clubs that center cultural wisdom and healing

When we build together, we amplify impact. A collective legacy is more than the sum of its parts—it's a vision carried by many hearts.

Spiritual Legacy and Inner Wisdom

Your legacy is also about how you've grown spiritually. What lessons have life and leadership taught you about love, courage, faith, and purpose? What practices sustained you? What beliefs shaped you?

Consider leaving behind not just what you did, but how you lived:

- A collection of spiritual reflections
- A ritual or prayer you created
- A philosophy of life you hope your loved ones will carry forward
- A "values will"—a document outlining your hopes and blessings for future generations

Spiritual legacy is subtle but powerful. It's the energy you bring into a room, the blessing behind your words, the guidance in your silence.

Legacy as Liberation

Living into your legacy is an act of liberation. It's the choice to reclaim your voice, honor your roots, and leave something intentional behind. You don't need a big stage. You need a bold heart.

When you live as your whole self, you free others to do the same. When you share your light, you become a lighthouse. When you document your wisdom, you become a well of guidance. Your legacy is your living proof that healing, thriving, and joy are possible—even after challenge, loss, or change.

Journaling Prompts: Crafting Your Legacy

- What stories do you want future generations to know?
- What values have guided your decisions?
- Who are the people or communities you want to impact most?
- What's one small act you can do today to begin shaping your legacy?
- If you had one final message to share with the world, what would it be?

Final Thoughts

You are not done. You are deepening.

This chapter of your life isn't about winding down—it's about rising up to offer the full measure of your wisdom, creativity, and love.

Let your legacy be one of courage, clarity, and compassion. Let it be bold. Let it be healing. Let it be yours.

You are the ancestor someone has been waiting for. And the legacy you leave will be more than a memory—it will be a map.

15

Letter to My Sister

To the Sister Who's Tired

"Rest is not weakness. Rest is remembering that you are more than what you do. You've done enough. You are enough."

Dear Sister,

I know that weariness. The kind that doesn't just live in your body, but in your bones. In your spirit. In the places that have held too much for too long.

You've done what was asked. And then some. You've led. You've held space. You've shown up when no one else did. And now, here you are—exhausted, wondering if rest will ever come.

Let me tell you: it will. And more importantly, *it must.*

Rest is not selfish. It's not a luxury or a sign of weakness. It's sacred. Necessary. Deserved.

You don't have to keep pushing. You don't have to keep proving. You don't have to earn your rest. You are worthy of softness just as much as you are worthy of strength.

There's no trophy for exhaustion. No prize for burnout. You don't owe anyone your depletion.

You have given enough.

Now it's time to receive. To be poured into. To be held—not just by others, but by yourself. By stillness. By silence. By Spirit.

Let your body exhale. Let your mind quiet. Let your soul stretch out into spaciousness.

You are allowed to unplug. To be unavailable. To take the nap. To sit in the sun. To stop explaining why you need a moment to just *be*.

This rest will not make you less. It will return you to yourself.

With deep respect and quiet blessing,

Your Sister Who Understands the Cost

16

Embracing Joy, Play & Restorative Living

"Rest is not retreat—it's reclamation. Joy is not a detour—it's the way home to ourselves."

Choosing Joy on Purpose

Joy is not frivolous. It's not a luxury or a reward to be earned after working hard enough. Joy is a birthright. A spiritual necessity. A guiding light in this next chapter of your life.

For too long, we've been taught that rest must be earned, that pleasure is indulgent, that ease is laziness. But what if joy is one of the most sacred expressions of a well-lived life? What if restoration is not the absence of productivity but the foundation of true purpose?

In retirement, joy is not only available to you—it is required.

The Winter Season: A Space for Possibility

There is a season for every part of life. If your career was your spring and summer—times of building and growing—then this new chapter is your winter. Not barren, but *pregnant* with possibility.

As we sit in our "winter" experience, we're invited to release old ideas, emotions, and activities that are no longer serving us. We make space for what is bubbling to the surface—new dreams, hidden talents, long-forgotten passions.

This is the season of integration. Of wholeness. Of turning inward to discover what's truly meaningful.

Redefining Leisure

We live in a culture that celebrates the hustle. But in retirement, you have the rare gift of time—and the opportunity to redefine what it means to spend it wisely.

Meaningful leisure isn't about killing time. It's about savoring it.

- Taking long walks with no agenda
- Returning to music, dance, or art
- Hosting meals and lingering in laughter
- Exploring new places with curiosity
- Sleeping in without guilt

You can now prioritize pleasure. Not as a distraction, but as a declaration: *My joy matters.*

The Power of Play

Children are masters of joy. They laugh without reason. They dance without choreography. They create without fear of judgment.

What if you let your inner child come out to play?

- Try something silly and new: pottery, improv, watercolor, gardening
- Join a community choir or dance group
- Build a puzzle, fly a kite, ride a bike

Joy lives in the moments we let go of expectations. Permit yourself to delight in the simple, the spontaneous, the soulful.

Healing Through Movement

Movement is one of the most accessible and profound ways to restore joy and vitality. Not movement as punishment or perfection, but as *presence.*

Dance in your living room. Stretch in the sun. Walk barefoot in the grass. Practice yoga or tai chi. Let your body move not to fix itself, but to express itself.

Your body carries stories. Movement helps you release those that no longer serve you and embody new ones filled with freedom and delight.

The Joy of the Senses

Joy also lives in the senses:

- In the smell of jasmine tea
- The warmth of a quilted throw
- The sound of your favorite playlist
- The taste of something delicious made with love

Fill your days with small rituals of sensory delight. Slow down and savor beauty. This, too, is healing.

Create a joy altar with items that awaken your senses, such as shells, candles, feathers, oils, and photos. Let it remind you: life is not something to endure, but something to *enjoy.*

Stillness as Power

Stillness is not stagnation. It is space for clarity. A space for divine downloads.

Many women discover their truest insights in moments of silence, not in the boardroom, but in the backyard. Not in a meeting, but in meditation. Not in noise, but in nature.

Practice stillness daily:

- Begin the day with 5 minutes of breath and gratitude
- Sit with a question and allow the answer to rise
- Embrace the in-between space as a wellspring of revelation

You'll be surprised how often peace whispers when the world is quiet.

∗ ∗ ∗

Why Rest Is Revolutionary

To rest is to say:

My body is not a machine.

I am worthy even when I am still.

I refuse to prove my value through exhaustion.

I am not here to perform strength—I am here to live in wholeness.

In a world that profits from your burnout, choosing rest is a way to interrupt the cycle.

You stop replicating the patterns that drained your mother, your grandmother, your ancestors.

You begin to live differently, and that difference becomes your legacy.

This is not laziness. This is leadership.

What a Restorative Lifestyle Looks Like

A restorative lifestyle is not a vacation from life—it's a way of life. It's a deliberate commitment to rhythms, rituals, and relationships that nourish your entire being.

Here are some practices and examples to help bring this to life:

Rhythms of Rest

- **The Sacred Pause**: *Building "do nothing" moments into your day. Not scrolling. Not planning. Just being.*
- **Slow Mornings**: *Rising without alarm clocks, starting the day with breathwork, stretching, or silence.*
- **Evening Wind-Downs**: *Replacing screens with soothing rituals—tea, music, candles, foot soaks, prayer.*

Spaces of Restoration

- **Creating a Rest Nook**: *A chair by the window, a corner filled with pillows, a spot outside where you just breathe. A place to be without obligation.*
- **Tech Boundaries**: *Putting the phone away at certain hours. Turning off notifications. Claiming uninterrupted stillness.*
- **Visual Simplicity**: *Clearing clutter, softening lighting, bringing in natural elements that calm the nervous system.*

Restorative Relationships

Nourishing Community: Spending time with people who don't require performance. Those who let you be quiet, real, and fully human.

Saying No Without Guilt: Choosing rest over pleasing others. Honoring your bandwidth.

Sharing the Load: Delegating. Asking for help. Trusting that you don't have to do it all.

Rest as Creation

Rest isn't only sleep—it's creativity, delight, beauty.

- Dancing slowly in your living room
- Cooking with music and intention
- Walking without tracking miles
- Gardening, painting, or reading with no goal in mind

This is rest, too. Rest is any space where your nervous system sighs, I am safe. I am home.

The Spiritual Power of Rest

Rest is a return to the divine. It is where Spirit speaks. Where your intuition becomes clearer. Where guidance emerges.

Your rest might become a form of prayer:

- Lying down in silence and listening
- Journaling as a dialogue with the Divine
- Taking naps not because you're tired, but because rest itself is holy
- In rest, you remember you are not holding everything alone.

Try This: Create Your Rest Manifesto

Write 3–5 "truths" about what rest means for you in this season.

Examples:

- I rest because I am enough.
- I do not need to earn stillness.
- My legacy includes softness.
- I rest so I can remember who I am.
- Put it somewhere visible. Let it guide your decision**s.**

What Women Are Saying About Rest

"I stopped treating rest like a luxury and started treating it like my birthright."
— Tanya, 61

"I built my entire new rhythm around rest, and I've never felt more alive."
— Michella, 59

"My whole life changed when I began resting before I was exhausted."
— Lisa, 68

Journaling Prompts: Crafting Your Restorative Lifestyle

- What does rest look like in your life right now?
- What would a restorative lifestyle feel like in your body?
- Where can you begin to release urgency or over-functioning?
- What one rhythm could you build this week to support rest?

Final Thought

You were never meant to live in a state of survival. Rest is your inheritance. Restoration is your responsibility–to yourself, to your body, to your spirit, and to the generations that follow.

You don't just deserve rest–you embody it.

And when you choose rest, you change the world.

* * *

Creating Your Joy Practice

Joy isn't accidental—it's cultivated. Establish a daily or weekly practice that helps you reconnect with yourself.

Try a "joy journal":

- Write three things that brought you joy each day
- Note what activities light you up and which ones dim your energy
- Track how joy shows up in your body, spirit, and relationships

You'll begin to notice patterns, and from those patterns, you'll be able to make choices that center your joy more intentionally.

"Stormy or sunny days, glorious or lonely nights, I maintain an attitude of gratitude."
—Maya Angelou

Joy in Community: Shared Light

Joy expands when shared. Make space for communal joy:

- Plan a regular brunch or tea with women who uplift you
- Host a creative circle with music, stories, and laughter
- Celebrate your wins, no matter how small

Let joy be something you *invite* into your home—and into your relationships.

A Guided Visualization: Restoring Joy

Find a quiet space. Sit or lie down comfortably.

Close your eyes. Inhale slowly, deeply... and exhale.

Imagine yourself in a place where you feel completely at peace. It could be real or imagined—a beach, a garden, a sun-drenched room. Feel the warmth of that space.

See yourself there, completely at ease. No pressure. No deadlines. Just you. Free.

Ask yourself: *What brings me joy?* Let images arise—dancing, cooking, painting, mentoring, laughing.

Let your heart guide you. Breathe it in. Smile gently. Whisper: "I choose joy."

When ready, open your eyes. Journal anything that came up.

The Joy of Letting Go

> *"Simplicity makes me happy."*
> —Alicia Keys

Sometimes, the most radical thing we can do is choose joy and simplicity. Embracing joy means letting go:

- Letting go of comparison
- Letting go of urgency
- Letting go of roles you've outgrown
- Letting go of people who no longer honor your growth

This letting go is not loss—it's liberation. It's clearing space for what's next.

Joy grows in open space.

The Power of Spaciousness

> *"It's not the notes you play; it's the notes you don't play."*
> —Miles Davis

There's a sacred art to leaving space. To not filling every moment, every breath, every calendar block. Just like in jazz, where the pause between notes creates the mood, the tension, the beauty, so too in life, it's the space between our doing that reveals our depth.

We've been conditioned to believe that meaning comes from constant motion. That if we're not producing, proving, or planning, we're falling behind. But what if the most meaningful moments are the ones where nothing is happening, at least on the outside?

What if spaciousness isn't emptiness, but possibility?

* * *

Spaciousness as a Form of Freedom

To embrace spaciousness is to choose enoughness. To resist the urge to fill. To trust that your value is not in what you do, but in how you are.

Spaciousness might look like:

- Leaving room in your day for wonder or rest
- Saying no without guilt
- Sitting with a feeling instead of rushing to solve it
- Creating margin in your schedule—not just for emergencies, but for beauty
- Letting silence stretch, even in conversation

These moments allow the soul to breathe. They are not wasted—they are essential.

Spaciousness and Purpose

You do not have to fill every hour with impact to live a purposeful life.

Your purpose may emerge more clearly in spaciousness than in structure. When you pause, the whispers become audible. When you rest, your intuition sharpens.

Spaciousness creates room for spiritual clarity, for creative flow, for emotional healing.

In your next chapter, let spaciousness be part of your design, not as a void to avoid, but as a well to draw from.

Reflection Questions: Living with Spaciousness

- Where in my life do I feel overfilled, crowded, or rushed?
- What might open up if I let something go?
- What do I avoid in silence that might be worth listening to?
- How can I create beauty through less, not more?

* * *

Soul-Centered Joy

What brings you closer to the divine? What reminds you that life is sacred?

This is the time to live soul-first:

- Attend spiritual gatherings
- Sit under a tree and watch the sky
- Read poetry that stirs your spirit
- Let ritual become your rhythm

You are not retiring from life. You are returning to it—in its fullest, richest, most joyful form.

Journaling Prompts: Your Joy Map

- What does joy feel like in my body?
- When was the last time I felt truly playful?
- What did I love doing as a child that I've set aside?
- What does rest look like for me right now?
- How can I design a day that centers joy?
- Who or what in my life supports my joy, and who or what challenges it?
- What joy rituals or rhythms can I commit to this season?
- What kind of joy legacy do I want to pass on?

Final Thoughts

This chapter of life isn't just about rest—it's about radiance.

As we reflect on what lights us up, it's important to remember that our passions are not just mental curiosities—they are *embodied truths*. They live in our bones, our scars, our breath. As the late Womanist theologian and ethicist Dr. Katie Geneva Cannon so powerfully wrote:

> *"Our bodies are the texts that carry the memories, and therefore remembering is no less than reincarnation."*

In other words, purpose lives not only in what we do, but in how we've lived, what we've endured, and what we now feel called to make sacred. The body holds the truth long before the mind understands it. And when we reconnect to that truth, we don't just remember—we are reborn.

Let joy be your compass. Let pleasure be your prayer. Let rest be your revolution.

You are not what you produce. You are what you feel, what you create, what you love.

May your days be filled with music, your heart full of peace, and your soul wide open to delight.

You have earned this joy. Now live it. Fully. Unapologetically. Freely.

17

Spotlight: A Restorative Ritual for Wholeness

There are times when the mind won't quiet, when the heart feels heavy, when the body forgets how to exhale. In these moments, you don't need a plan—you need a pause. A way to come home to yourself. A sacred rhythm that reminds you: *I am still here. I am still whole.*

This is a simple wellness ritual—part prayer, part intention, part restoration. It is not about perfection. It's about presence.

Create this space for yourself. Often. Tenderly. Without guilt.

The Ritual: A Return to Self

You will need:

- A quiet space
- A journal or notepad
- A candle or source of light

- A small bowl of warm water (optional)
- A soft item that comforts you (blanket, shawl, etc.)

Step 1: Prepare Your Space

Turn off distractions. Light your candle. Wrap yourself in your chosen item. Let your space feel sacred. Whisper: *This is time for me. This is space for my healing.*

Step 2: Ground Your Body

Sit or lie down. Close your eyes. Place one hand over your heart, the other over your belly.

Breathe in through your nose slowly for four counts, and exhale through your mouth for six.

Repeat for five breaths. Let each exhale soften you.

Step 3: Speak an Intention

Say aloud or write one of the following (or create your own):

- "I release what no longer serves me."
- "I return to my own rhythm."
- "I am safe, I am enough, I am free."
- "Joy is my birthright. Rest is my right."
- "I trust the unfolding of my life."

Let the words anchor you.

Step 4: Water Blessing (Optional)

Dip your fingertips in the warm water. Gently touch your temples, your heart, your hands—wherever you carry tension. Imagine the water washing away weariness. Whisper: *I am renewed.*

Step 5: Write

Ask yourself:

- What am I feeling right now—physically, emotionally, spiritually?
- What is my body asking for today?
- What small act of care can I offer myself this week?

Write freely. No judgment. No edits. Let your soul speak.

Step 6: Close With Gratitude

Blow out the candle. Place your hand over your heart again. Say:
*Thank you, body. Thank you, spirit. Thank you, breath.
I am here. I am home.*

Final Blessing

May you return to this ritual as often as you need.

Let it be a soft landing. A sacred mirror. A rhythm that brings you back to yourself when the world tries to pull you away.

You are not just transitioning. You are restoring. Reclaiming. Rising.

And you are worthy of that care, always.

IV

Your Journey, Your Rules

You've made it to the end—but in truth, this is only the beginning. What you hold in your hands is not just a book—it's a map. A mirror. A manifesto. It's a permission slip to live the rest of your life with radical joy, clarity, and intention.

18

Letter to My Sister

To the Sister Leaving a Legacy

"Your impact cannot be measured in titles. Your presence is your legacy. You have already changed the world in ways you may never see."

Dear Sister,

You may not realize it, but you're already leaving a legacy.

Not just in what you've accomplished, but in how you've lived. In the courage you've shown. In the lives you've touched. In the rooms you've walked into and quietly changed just by being fully yourself.

Legacy isn't only about monuments, foundations, or big stages. It's in your laughter. Your wisdom. Your care. The way you speak truth in love. The way you make space for others to rise without shrinking yourself.

It's in the stories you share. The recipes you pass down. The way you sit with someone when they need to be reminded of their worth. It's in your softness and your fire. In your prayers and your presence.

You don't have to try harder to make an impact. You already are one.

And yet, this season invites you to go deeper. To decide what you want to offer now—intentionally, joyfully, from a place of fullness. You have so much to give, not because you owe it to the world, but because your spirit is still overflowing with purpose.

Your lived experience is medicine. Your story is a map. Your becoming is a beacon.

So take your time. Listen inward. Ask yourself, *What do I want to be remembered for? What do I want to pass on?*

Then begin. One seed at a time. One story. One gesture. One brave offering.

Because you, my sister, are a legacy in motion.

With reverence and love,

Your Sister Witnessing Your Becoming

19

Conclusion

You've walked through transitions. You've reflected on identity, purpose, joy, and legacy. You've honored what was and dreamed into what could be. And now, you stand at the threshold of a life entirely shaped by your unique design. One that reflects your soul, not just your resume.

There is no single blueprint for what comes next. And that's the beauty of it. You are free. Free to choose. Free to explore. Free to define every day on your own terms.

Permission Granted

You don't need permission to slow down. To rest. To rise. To reinvent. You already carry the wisdom, the grace, and the power to do so. You've always had it. Maybe you forgot. Maybe the noise of the world made you doubt it. But it never left you.

Now is the time to claim it fully.

This season is not a retreat—it's a return. To self. To soul. To the dreams you paused and the parts of yourself you silenced in order to survive. Bring them all forward. They are part of your story. And your story still matters.

You are not disappearing. You are re-emerging. And this time, you get to come back home to yourself.

This Is a Sacred Season

This chapter is not a second act—it's a sacred one. It is not about doing more. It is about being more. More rooted. More radiant. More real. More rested.

You've earned the right to be discerning with your energy. You've earned the wisdom that comes from experience. And you've earned the joy of building a life that serves your spirit, not just your title.

Retirement, transition, or whatever you want to call this phase of life, is not about winding down. It's about rising up.

Rising into your wholeness. Rising into your brilliance. Rising into your calling—on your terms.

Living with Intention and Delight

Let this be your invitation to craft a life of deep satisfaction and daily joy. A life where rest is sacred, connection is intentional, and your days reflect your heart.

Living with intention doesn't mean having all the answers. It means listening.

CONCLUSION

To your body. Your intuition. Your longings. Your boundaries.

Living with delight means:

- Letting yourself laugh out loud
- Moving through the world with ease and wonder
- Trusting that the good things are meant for you, too
- Saying yes to beauty, softness, and soul

You don't need to ask for it. You get to choose it. Right now.

Take the First Step

Every journey begins with a single step. Maybe it's a conversation you've been meaning to have. A project you've longed to start. A trip you've dreamed of taking. A boundary you're ready to hold.

Start there. Start small. Start with what feels true.

There is no deadline. No scorecard. No need to compare. Just you, walking your path, surrounded by the wisdom of every woman who has come before you and every sister rising with you now.

Write one page. Make one call. Light one candle. Start one practice.

Small steps, taken consistently, become a rhythm. A way of life. A new legacy.

Stay Rooted in What Matters

As you move forward:

- Stay curious.
- Stay grounded.
- Stay joyful.
- Stay connected to your values and community.
- Stay centered in your body, your breath, your spirit.

Let joy be your compass. Let legacy be your intention. Let rest be your rhythm. Let love lead the way.

Be fierce in your clarity. Be soft with yourself. And above all, be devoted to what matters most to you, not what others expect.

Build Your Sanctuary

You don't have to go far to find peace. You can build a sanctuary right where you are.

Make your mornings sacred. Turn your bath into a ritual. Let your living space reflect your spirit. Hang art that inspires you. Play music that moves you. Create altars that honor your ancestors, your dreams, and your essence.

This life is yours to shape. Don't just live it—*curate* it.

CONCLUSION

A Blessing for the Journey

May you trust yourself more deeply than ever before.

May you know that your worth is not up for negotiation.

May you find beauty in your becoming.

May your days be full of grace, laughter, and unexpected delight.

May you speak your truth boldly and love yourself fiercely.

May you rest when needed, rise when called, and dance as often as possible.

May your heart remain open, your mind free, and your spirit sovereign.

And may you always remember: You are not what you do. You are who you are becoming.

You are not retiring from life. You are returning to it—in its fullest, richest, most joyful form.

What Comes Next

This book is the beginning of a conversation. With yourself. With your sisters. With your spirit. Let it be a spark that ignites something deeper.

Consider:

- Starting a journal practice to continue exploring your next chapter

- Hosting a small gathering or circle to discuss the themes in this book
- Sharing what you've learned with someone just beginning their own transition

Your journey matters. Your wisdom is needed. And your voice—your beautiful, powerful voice—is part of the song the world still needs to hear.

Final Words

You are the author of this next chapter. Write it boldly. Write it joyfully. Write it in your own voice.

No more waiting. No more shrinking. No more doubting.

This is your life. Your season. Your sacred becoming.

Your journey. Your joy. Your rules.

And sister, the best is yet to come.

A Circle of Voices

There's something sacred about sitting in a circle—no head, no tail, no hierarchy. Just women, sharing truth, passing wisdom hand to hand. A circle holds space for each voice to matter. It reminds us that we are not alone, and we never have been.

In this spotlight, I want to offer you a chorus of voices—reflections, affirmations, and wisdom from women who are walking this path too. Their stories are not all the same. Their lives are not identical. But each carries a thread of insight that might echo in your spirit.

Because sometimes what we need most is to hear from someone who's just a little further down the road.

> "You should think ahead and not just retire from something, you should retire from something to something."

—Lillian Lincoln Lambert, *Entrepreneur, Trailblazer, and Author of* The Road to Someplace Better

> "The 30's for women of color is a transitional period where you gain a different maturity about yourself... So when we hit our thirties, it's basically we stop and we say, wait a minute, why am I doing this?"

—Sueanne Pacheco, *Speaker, Storyteller, and Guide*

> "You don't get Steel from iron without going through a forge. You

don't get a diamond without going through the pressure that coal goes through. So you want to be that 24-carat diamond, you'll go through a change but it is possible to go through a change without just disintegrating."

—Dr. Tayo, *Menopause Advocate and Strategist*

"Thinking about the ways in which we navigate these points throughout our life really has a lot to do with how we understand self... and the ways in which we don different types of strategies in order to the best of our ability to mitigate harm to our soul and harm to our own reputation.

"... Liminality is always before us, and it is, how do we understand, ..., how do we avoid harm on our soul?"

—Rev. Dr. Angela Sims, *first woman president of Colgate Rochester Crozer Divinity School*

"Don't call me 'Senior' - I'm a vibrant, energetic, sexy, fearless OGC (older generation chick)! Now that I'm on my third entrepreneurial adventure, I'm ready to dance like I did 30 years ago, give more than ever, and take more risks without fear. I'm worth it!"

—Val Vick, The Luxury Retreat Architect

The advice I have comes from Proverbs 3:5, "Trust in the Lord with all your heart and lean not on your own understanding;" The path may not be clear to us, but we should trust the process, seek guidance through prayer and good counsel from mentors/coaches.

—Dr. Gloria Solomon, Purposeful Leader Coach

A young widow once told me that life is about learning to let go and live with loss in all of its forms. As a cancer survivor, I've learned to lean into gratitude—for the good, the bad, and even the awful—and to soften around pain and sorrow, savor joy, and then let them all go. Everything is impermanent, so I prioritize joy and shame-free rest.

— Andrea

Give yourself permission to evolve—drastically and unapologetically. Every new season is an opportunity to show up bigger, bolder, and more in alignment with your true purpose, even when it feels uncomfortable or unfamiliar.

— Toni Harris Taylor, Drastic Results Marketing and Sales Coach

These voices are only a few of many. You likely have your own words, your own stories, your own mantras that guide you.

You, too, are part of this circle.

You belong here—not because of what you've done, but because of who you are.

Try This: Start Your Own Circle

Whether virtual or in person, gather a group of women transitioning out of leadership, and ask these questions:

- What are you letting go of right now?
- What are you reclaiming?

- What do you want your legacy to feel like—not just look like?

There's medicine in every story. Healing in every shared truth. You never know what your voice might unlock for someone else.

An Invitation

Join the Conversation

And Be Part of a Soulful Community of Women Redefining What Comes Next

This is more than a book.

It's a doorway into a living, breathing conversation—one that continues long after the final page.

At pamelajthomas.com, you're invited to gather with women who are:

- Reimagining Life After Leadership
- Listening to the wisdom of their bodies
- Reclaiming joy, rest, creativity, and purpose
- Designing a new legacy—on their own terms

Each week, you'll receive reflections, roundtable invitations, podcast episodes, and soul-nourishing prompts that extend the spirit of *Women Don't Retire* into everyday life.

Come rest, reflect, and rise with us.

Join the community at: pamelajthomas.com

Let this be the beginning of your next chapter—one that unfolds in rhythm with who you are becoming.

About the Author

Where Spiritual Calling Meets Practical Wisdom

For many years, people asked me the same question: *"When are you going to seminary?"* I resisted. I already had degrees, certifications, and decades of experience—I didn't think I needed more education. But sometimes, life calls us into deeper alignment. In the mid-2000s, I finally said yes and stepped into seminary—not to become someone new, but to root more fully into who I had always been becoming.

That calling didn't arrive out of nowhere. My spiritual foundation was shaped early. My family's religious journey is one of curiosity, evolution, and quiet revolution. My father, the son of a Pentecostal minister, initially rejected religion when he moved to the U.S. for college and medical school. But everything shifted in 1969 when my mother brought us to a New Thought Unity Center. She wanted a place where we kids could go to Sunday School—and it turned out to be a turning point for our entire family. We children loved it. Eventually, my father joined us and found a theology that honored both his scientific mind and personal experience of the Divine.

That moment sparked a spiritual legacy that now spans generations. In 1977, my father founded the first New Thought church in Bermuda, and he was later ordained as a New Thought minister. My upbringing, while deeply rooted in faith, was more spiritual than religious, grounded in principles of openness, self-inquiry, and reverence for the sacred in everyday life. I was raised to believe that each person's spiritual path is valid and worthy, and that truth can be found in many traditions.

It's always stayed with me that my Pentecostal grandfather—so rooted in his tradition—was the one who first gave my father New Thought books. He showed up at my dad's church whenever he could, embodying the kind of openness that has guided my journey. My uncle Harold, my father's brother, was ordained in the Presbyterian tradition and pastored a Methodist-Presbyterian church before his untimely passing. A reconciliation center in Kansas City was later named in his honor. These are the threads that wove my understanding of ministry—not as dogma, but as presence, healing, and service.

Seminary gave me language for what I'd already been living. I encountered Womanist theology and a wider lens for experiencing the Divine. For me, ministry isn't just about preaching—it's about walking with people through transitions, thresholds, and transformations.

That spiritual depth is inseparable from my practical experience. I spent years as a financial advisor, walking alongside clients as they navigated questions not just of money, but of meaning. I've seen firsthand how financial decisions are entangled with identity, legacy, and emotional well-being. Over time, I became known not only for helping people manage wealth, but for helping them heal their relationship with it.

I believe true abundance includes both financial stewardship and spiritual alignment. That's why I approach wealth work as soul work—because money without meaning always leaves us searching.

A Lifelong Path to Wellness

Wellness, too, has been a thread that has been woven through my life. My father, as an OB/GYN, taught me to respect both conventional medicine and alternative approaches. That early exposure sparked a deep curiosity about healing that has only grown with time. As I faced my own health challenges, I turned toward therapeutic practices that honored the wisdom of the body.

Today, I'm certified in several healing modalities, including postural alignment and restorative movement. These aren't just techniques—they're invitations back to wholeness. My work blends movement, mindfulness, and soul-centered practices that allow people to feel seen, held, and restored.

What I've Learned

Through all of these paths—finance, ministry, healing—I've come to hold two enduring truths:
  1. Money without meaning cannot satisfy the soul
  2. Healing begins when we listen inward, not chase outward validation

Years ago, I had a dream where I heard a voice say, *"How do you start a revolution?"* The answer came immediately: *"One person at a time."* That dream became my mission.

Where I Am Now

Today, my work is about helping others remember what they already know—that their lives have sacred value, that transitions can be holy, and that wellness is our birthright. Whether I'm guiding women of color through the process of releasing old identities, teaching rest as resistance, or facilitating soul-aligned financial empowerment, I remain rooted in this truth:

We heal when we honor both the body and the spirit.

We grow when we reclaim our stories.

We lead when we live in alignment with our purpose.

And that, to me, is the real work of transformation.

****

Pam's specialty is getting to the core of what blocks our alignment – the limiting beliefs and programming that create stress, procrastination, sabotage, and even chronic physical pain, rather than progress, expansion, and expression. Imagine if you could find out exactly what's holding you back...and let go of it! Once past our blocks, Pam passionately believes that within all of us lies untapped potential, just waiting to be rediscovered.

With a rich background as a financial advisor and spiritual guide, she brings decades of experience to her work, offering unique insights into the stewardship of money and the spiritual dimensions of wealth. Her work is meticulously designed to assist visionary leaders in overcoming obstacles, re-energizing their purpose, and attracting the resources needed to create a positive impact in the world.

She teaches her clients how to tap into their inner wisdom for higher levels of creativity, inspiration, and courageous action (or finding a higher purpose in life).

Through individual coaching, workshops, and her videos, Pam helps clients calibrate and supercharge their alignment. Her workshops, programs, and private sessions are tailored to help visionary leaders get unstuck and re-energized to attract the people and resources needed to create the world they want to live in.

You can connect with me on:

- https://pamelajthomas.com
- https://facebook.com/pamela.j.jthomas
- https://www.linkedin.com/in/pamelajthomas

Subscribe to my newsletter:

- https://womendontretire.com/newsletter

Also by Pamela J. Thomas

He Restores My Soul
The Psalms are perhaps the most well-known and beloved book of the Bible. We sing the words in song and recite them as poetry.

Many of us think of faith as an intellectual exercise in which we affirm certain beliefs and principles. Some of us think of faith as our actions. The Book of Psalms reminds us that our walk with God is an emotional journey wrought with soaring highs and devastating lows. These words allow us to explore these emotions fully, by not attempting to hide or deflect from our pains and our joys, but instead diving headfirst into the feeling aspects of faith. These verses celebrate with us in times of overwhelming joy and offer solace during the darkest night of the soul.

Retirement By Design
If you have been anxiously wondering about the end of your career and what's next, this is the book for you. There is no need for you to keep delaying your retirement because you are unsure of the steps to take to have a smooth transition.

Instead of being immobilized by uncertainty, you can make a different choice. Retirement is an opportunity to live your passion, refine your purpose and establish your imprint on our world!

www.ingramcontent.com/pod-product-compliance
Lightning Source LLC
Chambersburg PA
CBHW062109080426
42734CB00012B/2808